IMAGES OF WAR
THE EIGHTH ARMY
IN NORTH AFRICA

PHOTOGRAPHS FROM WARTIME ARCHIVES

The Africa Star campaign medal was instituted on 8 July 1943. Awarded to any of the British or Commonwealth forces who served in North Africa between 10 June 1940 and 12 May 1943.

IMAGES OF WAR

THE EIGHTH ARMY
IN NORTH AFRICA

PHOTOGRAPHS FROM WARTIME ARCHIVES

SIMON FORTY

Pen & Sword
MILITARY

First published in Great Britain in 2019 by
PEN & SWORD MILITARY
an imprint of
Pen & Sword Books Ltd,
47 Church Street,
Barnsley,
South Yorkshire.
S70 2AS

A CIP record for this book is available from the British Library.

ISBN 978 1 52672 379 6

Printed and bound by CPI UK

Pen & Sword Books Ltd incorporates the Imprints of Pen & Sword Aviation, Pen & Sword Maritime, Pen & Sword Military, Wharncliffe Local History, Pen & Sword Select, Pen & Sword Military Classics and Leo Cooper.

For a complete list of Pen & Sword titles please contact
Pen & Sword Books Limited
47 Church Street, Barnsley, South Yorkshire, S70 2AS, England

E-mail: enquiries@pen-and-sword.co.uk
Website: www.pen-and-sword.co.uk

Abbreviations

APCR Amour-piercing composite rigid
APDS Amour-piercing discarding sabot
CLY County of London Yeomanry
CP command post
DAK Deutsches Afrika Korps
FA field artillery
FJR *Fallschirmjäger* = German paratrooper
GFM *Generalfeldmarschall* (Field Marshal)
KG *Kampfgruppe* = battle group, usually named for its commander.
LRDG Long Range Desert Group
OB West *Oberbefehlshaber West* = C-in-C West
OKH *Oberkommando des Heeres* = Army High Command
OT Organisation Todt
PIR parachute infantry regiment
PzGr *Panzergrenadier* = armoured infantry
RCT regimental combat team
SdKfz *Sonderkraftfahrzeug* = special purpose vehicle
TD tank destroyer—could mean towed ATk guns or tracked (M10, M18 or M36)
WDF Western Desert Force

Photographic Sources

The photographs in this book are predominantly from the collection of my late father, Gorge Forty; others are sourced via Battlefield Historian, from National Archives, College Park, MD or from the British Official photos in the collection of Martin Warren. The commnications images on pp105–107 are from the Signals Museum at Blandford. The maps and charts are by Mark Franklin, save the US official maps are from the various "Green Books" which can be found online at the US Army Center of Military History.

Contents

It was all palm trees,
Roman remains and
solar topees, wasn't it?

Introduction

The desert war has a peculiar place in the history of World War II. For the British it was a turning point. Churchill's 'before Alamein we never had a victory; after never a defeat' may be inaccurate but it catches the mood well. Victory over the Desert Fox and his Afrika Korps exploded the myth of Nazi invincibility, and provided Britain with a general to be proud of. The arrival of American troops in North Africa followed a few months later with the surrender of Axis forces in Tunisia was a successful start to an Allied partnership that would end with complete victory over Germany two years later.

For the Germans, the campaign in North Africa started as a sideshow, a holding action that took place against the backdrop of the invasion of Russia. Sent to help out their hapless Italian allies who were being comprehensively defeated by the British, the two understrength divisions under Rommel's command would swell to an army by the time the German forces surrendered. The supposed sideshow became a major drain on German resources that could have been better used in Russia.

The desert war is often talked of in terms of chivalry: that it was a war fought without the murderous excesses seen in other theatres. This is, of course, poppycock: no wars that involve aerial or artillery bombardment of populated areas can be described as chivalrous. There are always innocent casualties. Both sides treated the civilian population – particularly the Arabs – at best with indifference. In the desert, the German Army may not have lost its moral compass completely yet – that would happen in Russia – and, helped by the fact that there were no SS contingents, there are few reports of German atrocities (there are a number laid at the Italians' door). But the Jewish populations of towns in North Africa were treated as elsewhere in the Reich, and were used as slave labour or deported to the camps.

And what of the Desert Fox? Rommel may not have been as obviously a Nazi as Hitler's other favourites, but he owed much to his close connection to the Führer. The idea of chivalry and the admiration of Rommel as a good German just doing his duty was wartime propaganda that was twisted postwar, particularly as NATO sought to rehabilitate the German army. That being said, however, there's no doubt that the desert war was fought in a different manner when compared to other campaigns. There really did seem to be a fellow feeling between the adversaries that didn't exist elsewhere – perhaps best exemplified in the way that *Lili Marlene* became the song of the campaign on both sides.

There's also no doubting Rommel's tactical abilities, honed during the French campaign of 1940. He was an excellent commander of armoured units and he certainly seemed to have the knack of putting his forces in exactly the right place at the right time. In this, he was helped considerably by two intelligence coups. First, the Italians' P Section of the *Servizio Informazioni Militare*, the military intelligence service, stole the US 'Black Code', used to encode highly detailed reports about the state of the war, troop movements and equipment prepared by Colonel Fellers, military attaché to the US embassy in Egypt. Between January and June 1942, *die gute Quelle* 'the Good Source' as Rommel called him, gave the Desert Fox first class intelligence.

Second, on 24 April 1942, Capt. Alfred Seebohm landed at Tripoli – complete with radio intercept platoons, a radio direction-finding platoon, and a group of cipher specialists. They would form the legendary 621st Radio Intercept Company that did so much to feed Rommel information picked up from lax British radio traffic. This lasted until mid-1942 when an Australian unit caught Seebohm too close to the front line and destroyed the 621st – but not before it seized paperwork that made it clear how much information the Germans were able to pick up through this monitoring. British radio procedure and use of codes improved so much that the Germans later said it became the best of the Allies after this date.

With two significant sources of electronic intelligence ended, suddenly Rommel's handling of the campaign became less prescient. That this moment occurred when his nemesis, Gen. Bernard Law Montgomery, took over Eighth Army proved doubly unlucky for Rommel. Montgomery was a general with a better strategic view than Rommel, indeed than most of the generals of World War II and the postwar armchair critics. For him logistics and a methodical approach to warfare were more important than extravagant armoured thrusts: showboating that looked good but didn't win wars. Under Montgomery there was no more see-sawing up and down the North African coastline – just an inexorable, remorseless assault that rolled up the Axis forces and led to a significant campaign victory. In this Monty was also helped by the arrival of modern, state-of-the-art equipment in the form of the M4 Sherman and British 6-pounder antitank gun. For so long the underdog in the arms race, at last Eighth Army could compete on a more level battlefield. They did so with a cosmopolitan gusto that only the polygot British Army could achieve, with contingents from the empire – Australian, Indian, New Zealand, and South African divisions – and elsewhere – the Free French and Poles.

Finally, no analysis of the desert war would be complete without mention of the much-derided Italians. The disastrous handling of the invasion of Egypt by Marshal Rodolfo Graziani in 1940 started the war in North Africa, and the decisive British victory at Beda Fomm saw a huge Italian army surrender. This gift to the British propaganda machine ensured that Italian military prowess would be the butt of

The Allies sustained 250,000 casualties (dead, wounded and missing/captured) in North Africa, the Axis over 475,000 including over 430,000 made prisoner.

jokes and smears throughout the war, in spite of the frequent examples of bravery, steadfast tenacity and resolve shown by poorly armed Italian troops during the campaign. Often left in the lurch by the Germans, they fought a number of brilliant rearguard actions during the retreat, and their Bersaglieri light infantry and Folgore paratroopers were elite combat troops. If one wants an example of Italian bravery one need look no further than the 1941 Alexandria raid by midget submarines.

The desert war provided the Western Allies with a much-needed shot in the arm, boosting confidence in a significant way. British Eighth Army was instrumental in this, and would go on to prove its worth in Sicily and Italy.

The boundary between Tripolitania and Cyrenaica falls roughly halfway between Tripoli and Egypt. This triumphal arch, the Arco Fileni, was built on the Via Balbia, the Libyan coastal highway and survived until the 1970s as a symbol of Italian colonisation.

Chapter One

Setting the Scene

Despite being much more preoccupied with immediate self-preservation from September 1939 to September 1940, the importance of the Middle East still loomed large in British strategic policy. The Suez Canal was not only Britain's vital link to India, the Far East, Australasia and its African possessions, but it also provided an alternative route to the Americas – so its protection was considered essential.

The main threat to the canal came from Italy, whose dictator, Benito Mussolini, sought to take advantage of Britain's weakness by expanding the Italian colonies of Cyrenaica and Tripolitania. He joined Germany by declaring war on Britain on 10 June 1940. By that time there were two massive Italian armies in Libya, 221,530 strong. Opposing them were a mere 36,000 British and Commonwealth soldiers who were merged to become the Western Desert Force (WDF) under the command of Lt-Gen. Richard O'Connor and C-in-C Middle East, Field Marshal Archibald Wavell. Although there was a general shortage of guns, tanks, ammunition and transport, these troops would soon prove their battlefield prowess, and would go on to form the core of what would become the Eighth Army.

Beginning with a five-day raid whose continuing success turned into the full-blown Operation 'Compass', the WDF defeated the Italian Tenth Army and pursued them to Beda Fomm and El Aghelia, capturing Tobruk and taking 138,000 prisoners, many tanks, guns and aircraft, before its own meagre equipment wore out and some of its best units, including 4th Indian Division, were transferred away, as was its replacement (the 6th Australian Division) and the 2nd New Zealand Division, destined for Greece.

Meanwhile, on 12 February 1941 the German General Erwin Rommel had arrived in Tripoli with what became the Deutsches Afrika Korps, to reinforce the beleaguered Italians. Initially consisting of the 5th Leichte (Light) Division (later redesignated 21st Panzer Division) and 15th Panzer Division, together they were known as Panzer Group Afrika. Also under Rommel's command were four infantry and two armoured (Ariete and Trieste) divisions of the Italian First Army.

Rommel hit the ground running. On 24 March he launched a limited offensive which completely surprised the British, who were caught out by the speed and ferocity of the attack and soon had their positions outflanked and overwhelmed at El Agheila, Mersa el Brega and Agedabia. The Axis advance continued apace – on 3 April Benghazi fell and by the 8th the whole of Cyrenaica, except for the port city of Tobruk. With a garrison of 36,000 British and Australian troops, Rommel knew it was a key objective to cater for German logistical resupply and consequently besieged it intensively. The lack of this resupply had an immediate effect. Fuel and ammunition shortages curtailed any further Axis advances.

At this point, Churchill intervened. He forced Wavell to send troops to Greece and then pushed him into action in North Africa earlier than Wavell wanted. The field marshal acquiesced, launching operations 'Brevity' (15–16 May 1941) and 'Battleaxe' (15–17 June). 'Brevity' was an attempt to strike at a perceived Axis weak point in the Sollum-Capuzzo-Bardia border area between Libya and Egypt, while the intent of 'Battleaxe' was the relief of Tobruk. Both were against prepared, defended positions and were fairly quickly stubbed out – at Halfaya Pass by Italian gunners – with heavy losses.

Following the failure of these final WDF operations the unfortunate Wavell was replaced as C-in-C Middle East by General Claude Auchinleck. In September 1941 there was a reorganisation of British forces and Eighth Army was created.

British forces in the desert were drawn from many different countries. This group – seen outside Benghazi Cathedral at Christmas 1940 – is from 4th South African Armoured Car Regiment. Behind them are their Marmon-Herrington Mk III armoured cars.

Above Benito Mussolini inspects his troops. Although often depicted as a buffoon, he was a brave Bersagliere in WWI who ended the war with 40 shards of mortar bomb in his body.

Below Classic postwar view showing a US transport aircraft – there's no doubt that American aid, initially materiel and later troops, played a huge role in the British success.

Cruiser Mk Is of 1st Royal Tank Regiment move towards the front in spring 1940.
Note the two sub-turrets armed with .303in MGs. The main armament is a 2pdr gun
that was effective against the Italian tankettes but of little use against the PzKpfw III
and IV.

Above 'Fox killed in the open.' That's what Gen Richard O'Connor sent to Wavell after the defeat of Italian Tenth Army. Here a 3rd Hussar light Mk VI unfurls a captured banner of the Italian Royal Army.

Below The Light Mk VIB had a crew of three and was armed with two machine guns – a useful reconnaissance tool in 1939 but hardly a tank.

Gen Sir Archibald Wavell (right) – C-in-C Middle East – and Maj-Gen Richard O'Connor, who was OC operations in the Western Desert, confer before the assault on Bardia, 5 January 1941.

The Führer and *Oberster Befehlshaber der Wehrmacht*
(Supreme Commander of the Armed Forces)
Führer Headquarters
11 January 1941

Directive No 22
German support for battles in the
Mediterranean area

The situation in the Mediterranean area, where England is employing superior forces against our allies, requires that Germany should assist ... Tripolitania must be held ...
    I therefore order as follows:

1. C-in-C Army will provide blocking forces sufficient to render valuable service to our allies in Tripolitania, particularly against British armoured divisions. Special orders for the composition of this force will follow.
... this formation will be transported to Libya ... from about February 20.

2. X Fliegerkorps will continue to operate from Sicily ...

4. Instructions for the chain of command of German forces engaged in North Africa ... and on the limitations which will be applied to the employment of these troops will be laid down by the OKW in cooperation with Italian Armed Forces staff.

5. ... the movement of the blocking force to Libya ... will require the bulk of German shipping.

signed
Adolf Hitler

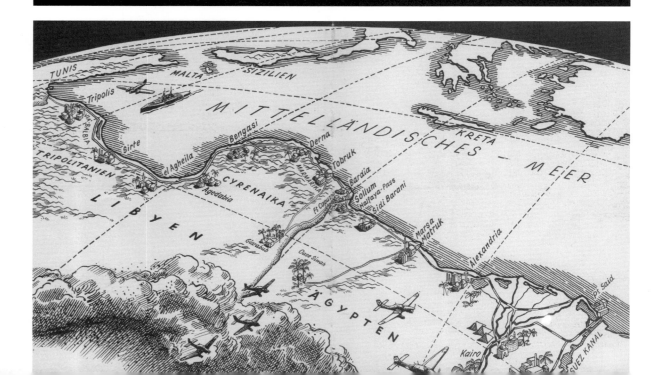

And then the Germans arrived. The mission statement was clearly laid out in Führer Directive No 22 (**left**): the strategy was to block the British, not attempt to take the Suez Canal. For all his brilliance in the field, Rommel neither had the troops nor the logistical tail to achieve this – although he gave it a good try. Problem was that by doing so he led to an escalation in men and equipment that was contrary to the German strategic aim. Note the German sketch map of North Africa and the location of Malta and Crete. The Germans took the latter with heavy casualties but were never able to subdue the former.

For a few brief weeks the Matilda II was called the 'Queen of the Battlefield.' Heavily protected and armed with a 2pdr gun which – in 1939–40 – was a heavyweight, the Matilda highlighted the British tank concept developed in the interwar period. Hidebound, riddled with complacency and dominated by the manufacturers, the British procurement system performed appallingly during the war. Too many poor decisions led to a range of tanks produced: light tanks for reconnaissance, infantry tanks – slow and heavily armoured and similar to their WWI predecessors – to be used to accompany the infantry; cruiser tanks were proposed for mobile operations. The concept may have looked good on paper – and Britain wasn't the only country to take up this approach. Indeed, the Germans used the PzKpfw III as a cruiser and the PzKpfw IV as an infantry tank: however, both German vehicles were easily and quickly upgunned and were more than a match for the British tanks.

Chapter Two
The Opposing Forces

The Desert Rats and the Afrika Korps are two units whose names have been taken in vain for 70 years. The creation of Eighth Army produced what would become the longest-serving British army of the war. It would fight through North Africa, Sicily and Italy, ending up in Austria in 1945. Its constituent elements included 7th Armoured Division – the original Desert Rats, whose shoulder insignia was a red jerboa (the natural desert rat) – but over the years the soubriquet has been extended to all those who fought in Eighth Army. The distinctive Desert Rat insignia is carried still by Britain's 7th Armoured Brigade.

The Deutsches Afrika Korps (DAK) had a much shorter lifespan, although it, too, lives longer in the memory. Created on 19 February 1941, on 15 August Rommel took charge of the renamed Panzergruppe Afrika, which was again renamed in January 1942 and became Panzerarmee Afrika. Later it became 1 Italienische Armee under Rommel's new Heeresgruppe Afrika, which changed leadership on 9 March 1943 when von Arnim took over. During this time – and to this day – the core of the German forces in Africa, 15th and 21st Panzer Divisions and the Afrika Division zbV, was the Afrika Korps, but the name tends to be used collectively to refer to German units in Africa.

In the early 1941 both British and German forces were small in number: German high command wanted merely to render the British ineffective in the Middle East until their great thrust into Russia was completed. Rommel's belligerence – and the steady build-up of British troops – ensured that this was not the case. Eighth Army when constituted had 2 corps and 6 divisions; by the end of the war in north Africa in 1943 the British had two armies in the field and Eighth Army had 3 corps, 11 divisions and 5 brigades. The German troops – as the DAK's name changes show – had similarly evolved into an army group.

The weaponry had also changed. The Allies had taken advantage of American weapons and benefited from the arrival of M3 Grants and M4 Shermans; German armour had more than kept pace, with the PzKpfw IV (special) – armed with a long 75mm main gun – proving itself to be more than a match for most earlier Allied tanks. The first PzKpfw VI Tigers were also introduced into battle at the end of the campaign.

There had also been two other significant changes to the Allied forces in North Africa: the first, the arrival of a British general Churchill would back to the hilt: Monty. Second, the introduction of US troops to the continent. Unsurprisingly, they struggled initially, but proved very quick learners.

British forces in Africa saw many changes of leadership, often because of the intervention of Prime Minister Winston Churchill (seen **Below Right** encouraging the troops in 1942). During Rommel's second offensive Eighth Army was led by Lt-Gen Ritchie (seen **Above**, L–R XXX Corps commander Lt-Gen Norrie, Ritchie and Lt-Gen Gott, at that time XIII Corps commander). Gott was Churchill's choice to replace Ritchie after the success of Rommel's second offensive, but his death led to the promotion of Montgomery.

Above Right One of Eighth Army's best divisional commanders, Lt-Gen Sir Bernard Freyberg had won the VC during WWI and led the New Zealand Division as pugnaciously as could be expected. Here he greets Foreign Secretary (and future prime minister) Anthony Eden.

Above Not at his best. It's 25 November 1941 and Rommel's troops are streaming westwards pushed back by Auchinleck's Operation 'Crusader'. Rommel is in his Horch staff car, his trademark goggles clipped to his cap. He found them when 'Max' and 'Moritz' were taken (see caption below). H.W. Schmidt in *With Rommel in the Desert* relates: when Rommel found them he took them saying, "Booty is permissable I assume; even for a general."

Below Three AEC Dorchester 4x4 ACVs (belonging to Maj-Gen Gambier-Parry, OC 2nd Armoured Division; Lt-Gen Sir Phillip Neame VC, OC Eighth Army; and Lt-Gen Sir Richard O'Connor, Neame's assistant commander) were captured by the Germans near Mechili on 7–8 April 1941. Dubbed the Mammuts, two were presented to Rommel's HQ. They were nicknamed 'Max' and 'Moritz' after characters in a children's story by Wilhelm Busch.

Above Rommel with GFM Albert Kesselring (German C-in-C Mediterranean). The Luftwaffe was critical to the success of the German ground forces in the campaign. Kesselring's first task on his arrival in theatre in November 1941 was to secure air cover for supply convoys to Africa – and that meant neutralising Malta. Kesselring was able to provide Rommel with the reinforcements he needed to go onto the offensive at Gazala and then took over command of Italian X and XXI Corps on 29 May 1942 when General der Panzertruppe Ludwig Crüwell was captured. Kesselring's nose was put out of joint when Rommel convinced Hitler that an attack on Egypt was more important than Kesselring's preferred attack on Malta. Kesselring was proved correct as Rommel's attack petered out with logistic problems.

Above The Humber Mk III boasted a turret armed with 15mm and 7.92mm Besa MGs.

Below The AEC Mk I armoured car was armed with a 2pdr gun in a Valentine turret. The Mk II (seen here) was upgunned to a 6pdr.

Above The Marmon-Herrington Mk II armoured car was armed with a Boys anti-tank rifle and a .303in MG. This is a late model Mk II and has an octagonal turret.

Below Morris CS9 armoured car of the 11th Hussars (the Cherrypickers). The parasol was not standard equipment!

Three shoddy tanks: the Cruiser Mk I (A9) (**Opposite, Below**) – this is a 1RTR tank; Cruiser Mk II (A10) (**Above**) – this one from 2RTR; and Cruiser Mk IV (A13) (**Opposite, Above**) – also from 2RTR. The cruiser tanks embodied much that was wrong with British tank design. Slow, poorly armoured and undergunned, the cruisers were badly out of the league of the PzKpfw IIIs and IVs who made mincemeat of them. Note the tanker's uniform: black beret, webbing belt and holster and one-piece tank oversuit (better known as the Pixie suit).

Below A15 Crusader Mk IICS armed with a 3-inch howitzer. There were a number of attempts to upgun and uparmour the Crusader, and the Mk III with a 6pdr gun was able to give a reasonable account of itself in 1942–43. This was important because there was no suitable replacement and it was more important to have tanks – even if they weren't very good – than none at all.

Above Right One of the big problems with the Crusader was its mechanical fragility ... and the lack of British expertise in battlefield recovery techniques – unlike the Germans. General von Ravenstein called the desert 'a tactician's paradise and a quartermaster's hell.'

Below Right The Matilda infantry tank was quickly overtaken by German upgunning. The 50mm-armed PzKpfw III and 8.8cm anti-aircraft/anti-tank gun could pick off Matildas before their 2pdr could get into range. The answer was to upgun with the 6pdr – but changing production from 2pdr to 6pdr would have reduced output at a critical time when quantity was seen as more important than quality. The Matilda soldiered on until a disastrous performance during the Gazala battles ensured it wouldn't be used in the desert again. Shipped to the Far East, it performed well against the Japanese whose anti-tank weapons weren't as powerful as those of the Germans.

America to the rescue! US equipment gave hope to British tank forces who were fed up with their weapons. The M3 Stuart (**Above**) light tanks may not have had much hitting power but they were reliable and the British loved them. The M3 light became the 'Honey' in British hands. Note the welded turret and riveted hull. Of more weight were the M3 mediums (**Opposite**) – the British dubbed those upgraded to have a turret with a radio and other improvements, the 'General Grant'; the US version, also used by the British, was the 'General Lee'. The 75mm sponson-mounted gun made a welcome difference and allowed the British armour to match the Germans for a while. It looked ungainly and posterity doesn't rate it highly, but it was better than anything else in the inventory until the M4 Medium came along. These two classic photos show well a range of details: the counterweight on the short-barrelled M2 main gun; the British commander's turret that mounted a 37mm gun; the attachment of canvas to the side of the tank to allow a bivouac to be quickly set up when in laager; and the crew of six.

Below and Inset Below The M4 Sherman first saw action at the second battle of El Alamein, one of US 4th Armored Division's regiments losing theirs to provide Eighth Army. It is rumoured that this unusual benevolence was partly induced by the embarrassment felt by Roosevelt following the discovery that the Axis powers were reading Fellers's reports. The height difference between the M3 and M4 mediums was considerable: the M3 Lee was 10ft 3in tall, the M4A1 with the rounded hull a mere 9ft. Additionally, the M4 could hide hull down with its turret-mounted main armament visible, whereas the M3 had to maintain its height to keep the sponson-mounted armament clear. The lack of counterweights mean that the Lees' main guns are M3s.

Inset Below 3CLY Sherman I seen in June 1943. Note the camouflage – blue/black over light mud. Note, too, the sand shields.

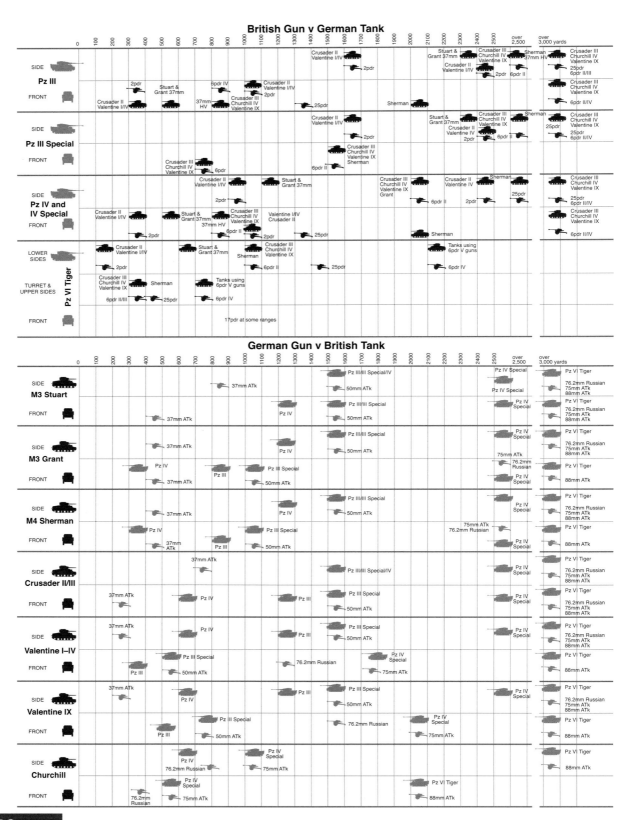

Comparison of British/Axis Armour and Anti-Armour Capabilities

Note: Width of shell as drawn indicates comparative weight of shell

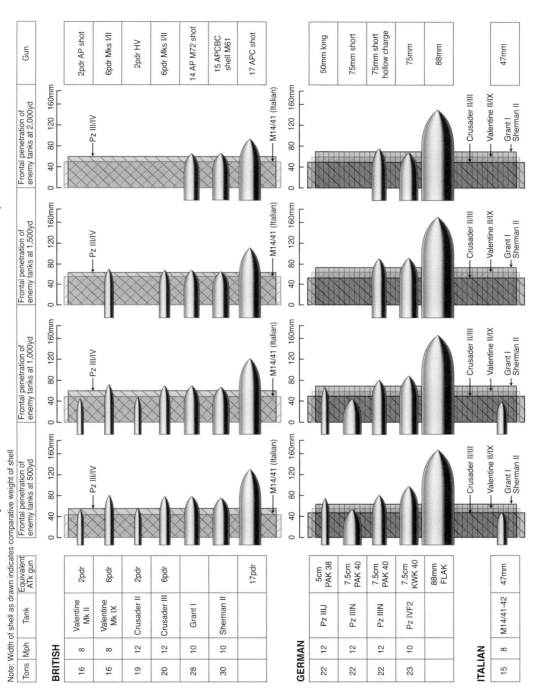

Gun
2pdr AP shot
6pdr Mks I/II
2pdr HV
6pdr Mks I/II
14 AP M72 shot
15 APCBC shell M61
17 APC shot

Gun
50mm long
75mm short
75mm short hollow charge
75mm
88mm

Gun
47mm

BRITISH

Tons	Mph	Tank	Equivalent ATk gun
16	8	Valentine Mk II	2pdr
16	8	Valentine Mk IX	6pdr
19	12	Crusader II	2pdr
20	12	Crusader III	6pdr
28	10	Grant I	
30	10	Sherman II	
			17pdr

GERMAN

Tons	Mph	Tank	Equivalent ATk gun
22	12	Pz IIIJ	5cm PAK 38
22	12	Pz IIIN	7.5cm PAK 40
22	12	Pz IIIN	7.5cm PAK 40
23	10	Pz IVF2	7.5cm KWK 40
			88mm FLAK

ITALIAN

Tons	Mph	Tank	Equivalent ATk gun
15	8	M14/41-42	47mm

37

Above The PzKpfw II – like the British Light Mk VIB – was obsolete by the start of the desert war. Armed with a 20mm gun, with a crew of three and a top speed of 25mph, it had been uparmoured from the Polish campaign.

Below Left and this page The PzKpfw III was an excellent tank that was uparmoured and upgunned throughout the campaign, starting with a 37mm and ending with a 75mm. The longer-barrelled 5cm KwK L/60 (**Below**) improved its hitting power considerably.

Two more PzKpfw IIIs, including an Ausf J (**Below**) with a longer-barrelled 5cm KwK L/60. These were called 'Specials' by the British because of their improved armament. At the start of the Crusader battles, the bulk of Rommel's armour was PzKpfw IIIs, with only around 20 of these being Specials, equipped with the longer-barrelled 50mm gun – 134 in the 15th and 122 in the 21st Panzer Divisions.

Above The PzKpfw III chassis was used to produce the Sturmgeschütz III, armed with a 75mm StuK37 L/24 gun. This one's an Ausf D.

Below PzKpfw III and Rommel's SdKfz 250/3 Greif command vehicle in the western desert at the time of the Gazala battles, 1942. Note the heavy frame on Greif – a radio aerial. *Bundesarchiv, Bild 1011-784-0246-22A / Tannenberg / CC-BY-SA 3.0*

Above Matilda II *Beutepanzer* – lit 'booty tank' – captured and impressed into German service, something both sides did a lot of during the campaign. A good example of this is the use of vehicles and stores by the Germans after they took Tobruk. The capture of these assets helped prolong Rommel's thrust eastwards.

Below Matilda in the background, PzKpfw IV in front. In March 1942 Rommel had 41 PzKpfw IVs, 22 in the 15th and 19 in the 21st Panzer Divisions.

Two views of a knocked-out PzKpfw IV Ausf G in Tunisia. While this one won't be recovered, many were and put back into service again. The Germans were better versed and better equipped than the British to do this.

Above This study of a PzKpfw IV shows off its Afrika Korps markings. Note the wishbone-shaped frame below the main gun. This was fitted on Ausf Ds and later short-barrelled versions to push down the radio antenna as the turret rotated.

Below Destroyed PzKpfw IV Ausf F2 outside Benghazi in 1942.

Opposite The Germans modified many outdated tank chassis to provide self-propelled artillery. The Czech PzKpfw 38t was used as the basis for the Marder (**Above** a Marder III). The PzKpfw I Ausf B was used for this 4.7cm PaK (**Below**) which saw service until 1943.

To begin with the main Italian tank used in the desert was the M13/40 (**Above**) which combined ease of manufacture and a decent armament – a 47mm Cannone da 47/32 M35 main gun, a coaxial 8mm Modello 38 MG and two other 8mm Modello 38 bow-mounted MGs in a ball mounting. The main gun proved adequate until 1942, although it had problems defeating the more heavily armoured Matildas and Valentines. Developed from this was first the M14/41 and then the M15/42 (**Left**) this one in the Saumur Tank Museum. The Italian 132nd Armoured Division – Ariete – fought well before being decimated at El Alamein while trying to cover the general retreat.

The Semovente 75/18 mounted a 75mm Obice da 75/18 modello 34 mountain gun and was the main fire support self-propelled gun in Italian armoured divisions. The chassis was initially that of an M13/40 butsubsequently the M14/41 and M15/42 were used.

Above Left Advancing Semoventi 75/18 from the Ariete Division, Libya, 1942.

Below Left The Semovente 75/18 at Saumur is named for the 133rd Armoured Division, Littorio, which arrived in theatre in January 1942. It fought well despite its poor equipment and was eventually sacrificed by the Germans as they retreated from defeat at El Alamein.

Above Note the vain attempts to improve the protection of this Semovente 75/18 using spare tracks and sandbags.

Above It may not have been on a par with the 88, but the QF 6pdr, which arrived in North Africa in April 1942, was powerfully effective when it arrived. Also taken up by the US (as the 57mm Gun M1) the 6pdr was capable of knocking out any German tank at the time. It fared less well against the new Tigers and Panthers until better ammunition was devised (APCR and APDS) and the first Tigers knocked out were destroyed by towed 6pdrs and Churchills of 48RTR equipped with the tank version.

Above The BL 4.5-inch medium gun, usually towed by an AEC Matador, was used by British artillery units throughout the war. It was an effective gun and could fire an 25kg HE shell over 11 miles.

Right British QF 3.7-inch AA guns at Tobruk. 51st (London) Heavy Artillery Regiment, RA was involved in the 240-day siege using its guns in both AA and anti-tank roles. In September 1941 it was taken out of the line, returning to the front line in March 1943 as part of the air defences of Tripoli.

Above The Ordnance QF 25-pounder, with limber (carrying 32 rounds), towed by a Morris Commercial 'Quad'. One of the most remarkable weapons of the war, the 25pdr served well into the postwar years.

Below It fired a lighter shell than other country's field artillery but it was accurate and speedily used by a crew of four to six. The 25pdr was used in the Bishop and Sexton self-propelled guns.

Both 2pdr (**Above**) and 6pdr (**Below**) antitank guns were used in the portee role, mounted on the back of suitable vehicles (usually 3-tonners such as the Austin K5 or Bedford QL). This gave the weapons excellent mobility but also meant that they and their crews lacked protection from small arms or shrapnel. They could be effective as at Sidi Rezegh when 2Lt Ward Gunn and and Maj Bernard Pinney of A Troop, J Battery, RHA held off a tank attack after which Gunn was awarded a posthumous VC and J Battery was given the honorific title 'Sidi Rezegh'.

The German 8.8cm dual-purpose anti-tank/anti-aircraft gun really was much better than any other weapon on the North African battlefield. Capable of firing 20 AP rounds a minute, it could knock out British tanks at ranges of up to 4,500 yards – greater than they were able to reply. It had an excellent sight and could be devastating. At the Halfaya Pass on 17 June 1941, for example, five 88s knocked out more than 80 British tanks. The gun was more than a match for any tank that was deployed in the theatre.

Comparison of Allied and Axis Artillery Capabilities

Weapon	Range in 000yd	Remarks
BRITISH		
18pdr gun	~9.6	
3.7in howitzer	~6.5	
4.5in howitzer	~6.2	
18/25pdr gun	~11.5	
25pdr gun/howitzer	~12.8	Also fired an AP shot
4.5in gun	~20.5	
6in howitzer	~11.2	
5.5in gun/howitzer	~16.5	
US 105mm SP howitzer	~10.8	M7 Priest mounted on a Grant chassis
7.2in howitzer	~16.6	
60pdr gun	~14.5	
3in Mk 5 mortar	~1.8	
4.2in mortar	~4.2	
GERMAN		
75mm lt inf gun	~3.8	Also fired hollow charge
150mm med inf gun	~5.1	
105mm lt fd howitzer	~12	Also fired AP, Tracer, hollow charge
105mm med gun	~20.7	
150mm med fd howitzer	~14.4	Also fired hollow charge
150mm gun	~18.3	
210mm howitzer	~26.6	
170mm gun	~32	Mounted on howitzer carriage
80mm 5GW34 mortar	~2.5	
150mm Nebelwerfer 41 mortar	~7.7	six barrels
210mm Nebelwerfer 42 mortar	~8.5	five barrels
ITALIAN		
47/32 gun (Med 35)	~3.6	Usual close SP and ATk gun of Italian Army
75/27 gun (Med 11/12)	~9	Also fired hollow charge
75/18 gun/howitzer	~10.4	Replacing 75/27 SP version on Mt13/40 chassis
100/17 howitzer	~10	Old Austrian design. Also fired hollow Charge
105/28 gun	~14.6	
149/23 howitzer	~9.6	
81mm mortar	~4.5	

Thickness of bar indicates relative weight of projectile

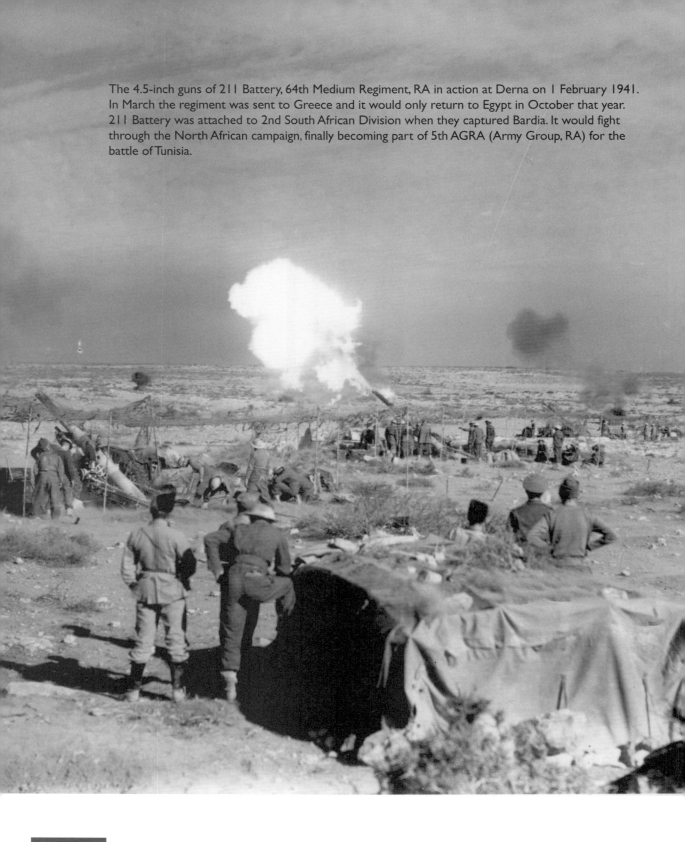

The 4.5-inch guns of 211 Battery, 64th Medium Regiment, RA in action at Derna on 1 February 1941. In March the regiment was sent to Greece and it would only return to Egypt in October that year. 211 Battery was attached to 2nd South African Division when they captured Bardia. It would fight through the North African campaign, finally becoming part of 5th AGRA (Army Group, RA) for the battle of Tunisia.

Chapter Three

Fighting in the Desert

The desert is an unforgiving environment to live in, let alone fight a war. The perils of getting stranded are obvious and are well exemplified by the story of the *Lady Be Good*, a B-24D Liberator that crashed in Libya in April 1943 – and only discovered by an oil exploration team in 1958. The bodies of eight of the nine-man crew, who had parachuted safely from the aircraft, were subsequently found nearly a hundred miles away. The co-pilot's diary tells a tragic story: their direction finder had broken and, thinking they were still over the sea when they bailed out, they tried to walk north to safety, with one small canteen of water.

Unsurprisingly, other than some special forces teams such as the Long Range Desert Group, most soldiers stayed away from the open desert and the armies fought along the corridor between the desert and the sea. Hot by day, cold by night, plagued by flies and other venomous creatures, most at first regarded the desert as the mouth of hell itself. Many, however, came to find a beauty in this grim landscape and this helps account in part for the fellow-feeling shown by those who fought there.

The *Lady Be Good* was well preserved after its crewless landing in the Libyan desert.

Above Siwa Oasis is in the heart of the desert but it changed hands a number of times during the campaign. There were few urban areas in North Africa so the fighting led to fewer civilian casualties than in other theatres.

Below Some of Arab populations of the area were pro-Nazi – in particular with regard to their anti-Semitic stance. Nazi labour camps in Tunisia, Algeria and Morocco killed over 2,500 Jews, but there was little violence between the Jews and Muslims. Anti-colonialism was certainly a significant factor in Arab allegiances, but on balance more Arabs assisted the Allies than fought against them. In Egypt, Britain employed 200,000 during the war.

The Qattara Depression is a large, low-lying area of soft sand and salt pans that was impassable for armoured vehicles and sizeable military units. Surrounded by cliffs and escarpments it was crossed by small specialist units (such as the LRDG) but was used to anchor the defences of the El Alamein line.

Above A sandstorm nears, and it can near quickly! Moving at over 25mph they last from only a few minutes to days. Blown sand and vehicles don't mix well together, and gritty lubrication caused much wear and tear.

Below Digging vehicles out of the sand was a perennial problem, as might be imagined.

Right A position in the Gazala line. Note the sacking covering the two rifles' working parts, the signal pistol behind and the knife and spoon on the sandbag in front.

Left Both sides laid extensive minefields – estimates put numbers at more than 22 million – to limit each other's movement. The 'Devil's Garden' between the two sides at El Alamein was five miles wide.

Above The invention of a workable mine detector made a significant difference. Lt Józef Kosacki produced a viable version based on earlier Polish work. Unpatented and gifted to the British Army (for which he received a letter of thanks from King George VI), 500 were quickly manufactured and rushed to Africa. They arrived in time to materially assist the British at El Alamein.

For obvious reasons, water is pretty important in the desert for men and machines. Rationed carefully in the field, a bath was a rare event and one to be savoured. One Royal Engineer remembered living for days with only enough water to rinse teeth: none for washing. Another remembers shaving in cold tea. Fuel cans were used to filter dirty washing water by boring holes in the base, filling it full of sand and using the sand as a filter.

Signal magazine showed the path of one jerrycan (water can No 4) from dock to front line. Designed in the 1930s and holding 40 litres, the jerrycan (the *Wehrmacht-Einheitskanister*) was significantly better than its British 4-gallon equivalent which were nicknamed 'flimsies' because of their propensity to leak after even the slightest knock. There was one advantage to this. They were easily adapted into Benghazi Burners – cooking stoves.

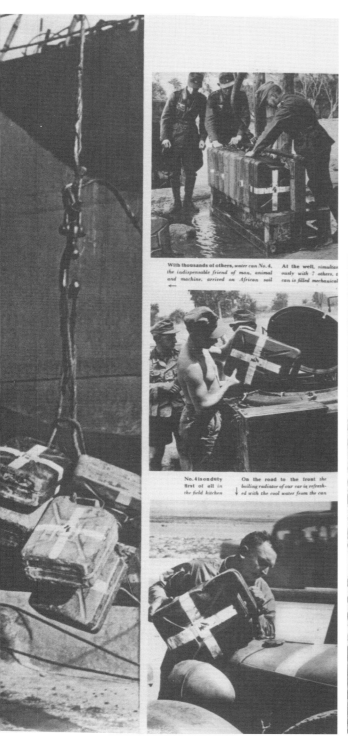

With thousands of others, *water can No. 4, the indispensable friend of man, animal and machine, arrived on African soil ←*

At the well, simulianously with ? others, s can is filled mechanical

No. 4 is on duty first of all in the field kitchen

On the road to the front the boiling radiator of our car is refreshed with the cool water from the can ↓

Camouflage was important in the desert, and was carefully used. Vehicles were either painted in a single colour (in 1940–41 that was mainly Light Stone No 61 or Portland Stone No 64). In late 1942 a wider range of colours was used including Desert Pink with a disruptive Dark (Olive) Green. These colours were changed when the army reached Tunisia.

Scenes of desert life – as with soldiers everywhere news from home and writing letters were essential requirements to maintain morale; so were decent shelters from the searing daytime heat and surprisingly cold nights. Personal hygiene was important: in the desert, sores or minor wounds often suppurated. Flies were a continuous plague, settling everywhere where there was moisture, including sweaty shirts and faces. There were more flies than mosquitoes, but the latter carried malaria. Examination of the figures in Morocco shows malaria increase year on year from 1939 (1,354 cases) to 1943 (6,233) but all this really shows is that the military measures to protect against an epidemic had been successful. Little yellow tablets – Mepacrine – kept the malaria rate down.

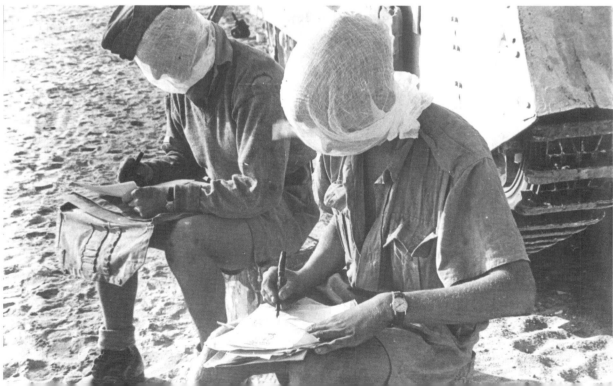

Above Left Crew of a Cruiser Mk I ready a laager to create as much shade as possible.

Left Always kip when you can, as exemplified by the crew of a Bedford MWD on column duties.

Above A rather stonier sleeping location.

Left and Below Left Posed shots, but they show well British infantry equipment. Note bayonets fixed on the Lee Enfields, magazine-less Tommy gun and Bren gun. The uniform comprises a khaki shirt, 'Bombay Bloomers' – baggy shorts – woollen socks, 1937 webbing with two large ammunition pouches, steel helmets and packs.

Below Vickers MG team from Z Company, 1st Battalion Royal Northumberland Fusiliers. Renowned for its reliability, the .303 MG, often water-cooled, was used in both world wars.

Above Eighth Army had a remarkable number of Commonwealth soldiers, and the Indian contingent included many Sikhs from the Punjab.

Below The Rajputana Rifles played a prominent role, winning two VCs, one in East Africa and the other, to Company Havildar Major Chhelu Ram, for bravery at Djebel Garci on 19–20 April 1943.

Above The Universal carrier was unique. No other army had a tracked vehicle like it. Entering service in 1934, it saw use throughout World War II often armed with Bren guns or Boys anti-tank rifles. An infantry battalion employed 20 in its mortar and carrier platoons.

Below French Spahis were equipped with armoured cars by the British and would later take part in the liberation of Paris.

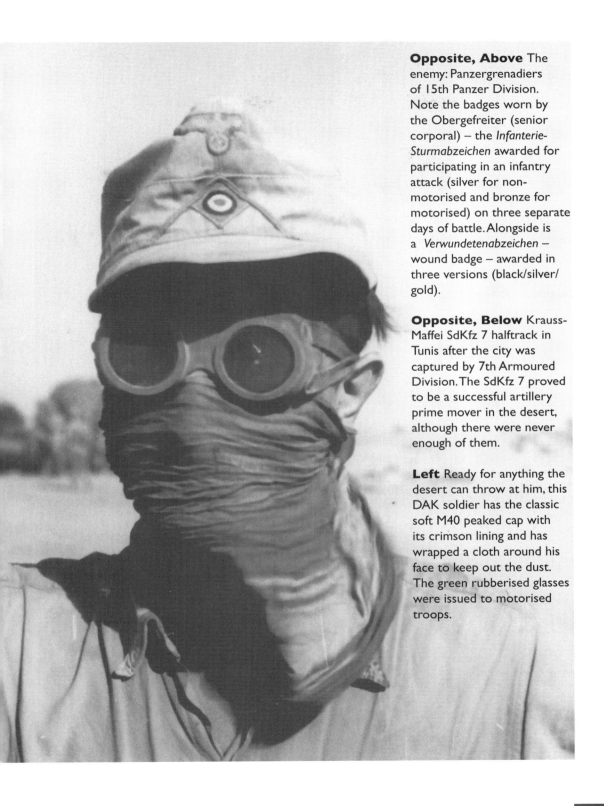

Opposite, Above The enemy: Panzergrenadiers of 15th Panzer Division. Note the badges worn by the Obergefreiter (senior corporal) – the *Infanterie-Sturmabzeichen* awarded for participating in an infantry attack (silver for non-motorised and bronze for motorised) on three separate days of battle. Alongside is a *Verwundetenabzeichen* – wound badge – awarded in three versions (black/silver/gold).

Opposite, Below Krauss-Maffei SdKfz 7 halftrack in Tunis after the city was captured by 7th Armoured Division. The SdKfz 7 proved to be a successful artillery prime mover in the desert, although there were never enough of them.

Left Ready for anything the desert can throw at him, this DAK soldier has the classic soft M40 peaked cap with its crimson lining and has wrapped a cloth around his face to keep out the dust. The green rubberised glasses were issued to motorised troops.

Opposite, Above Another halftrack artillery prime mover/recovery vehicle, the SdKfz 9 – the 'Famo' after the manufacturer of the first prototype, Fahrzeug und Motorenbau GmbH – had a 270hp 12-cylinder Maybach HL108 petrol engine and weighed a mighty 18 tonnes. Here one is pulling a 15.5cm sFH 18.

Opposite, Below The height of the 88 was a drawback if the enemy got close enough – but as most British tanks in the early days carried 2-pounders that didn't have HE ammunition, they'd be lucky to get close.

Above The Germans mounted many different types of gun on halftracks – including the 88 and various Flak weapons. This is a *7.62cm FK36(r) auf Panzerjäger Selbstfahelafette Zugkraftwagen 5t* (SdKfz 6/3) armed with a captured Russian 76mm F-22 gun in a 10mm casemate. Nine of these reached the desert battlefield in 1941 where the the British nicknamed them 'Dianas'. This one was captured by Eighth Army.

Above The SdKfz 2 kleines Kettenkraftrad HK 101 – usually known as a Kettenkrad – was a useful small all-terrain vehicle, here transporting wounded.

Below It was often cold in the desert, counterintuitive although that may seem. Jim Lucas remembers that you couldn't see the advancing infantry's legs when they were wearing greatcoats and they seemed to float towards you like Daleks.

Chapter Four

Operation 'Crusader'

The Eighth Army was formed in September 1941 under the command of Gen Sir Alan Cunningham from what remained of the WDF along with fresh equipment and reinforcements. (See organisation table with names of commanding officers on page 82.) It was comprised of two corps – XXX and XIII. XXX Corps consisted of six divisions all of which were bursting with new equipment – 300 cruiser tanks, 170 infantry tanks and 300 of the new American lend-lease M3 light tanks. Also 34,000 lorries, 600 artillery pieces, 240 AA guns, 200 anti-tank guns and 900 mortars. Of course, quantities of vehicles – new or otherwise – doesn't lead to success. While the British may have dubbed the M3 light the 'Honey' because of its reliability, it was still a light tank armed with a 37mm main gun. That may have been a match for the Italian M13/40, but it was no contest for the German tanks.

Immediately Auchinleck launched Operation 'Crusader' (18 November 1941– 31 January 1942) to relieve Tobruk. Although ultimately successful in this aim, and in pushing the Axis forces east to El Agheila, the offensive served to highlight the problems that the British had in integrating and coordinating their armour, infantry and artillery. At the start of the operation Eighth Army outnumbered the combined Axis force 118,000 to 113,000 men, with 680 tanks and 500 more in reserve against Rommel's 390 and with over a thousand aircraft against the Luftwaffe's 320. However, fighting against high quality German armour, the excellent anti-tank capability of the 88mm and battle-hardened troops, tactical deficiencies proved costly in both men and materiel. It was just as well that British logistics coped with the high attrition rate better than the Germans.

British 70th Division (also incorporating Polish troops) was shipped in to Tobruk to replace the beleaguered Australians, and on 18 November XXX Corps advanced through the southern desert, intending to seek out and destroy enemy armour before turning northwest to link up with the 70th Division which was instructed to attempt a breakout. After initial success these attempts faltered and by 21 November both units were pinned down by intensive artillery fire from Rommel's 90th Light Division. The situation was rescued by the advance of XIII Corps, which engaged the enemy positions along the coast on 22 November and whose New Zealand Division won through at Sidi Rezegh, forcing a corridor between Tobruk and XXX Corps by

EIGHTH ARMY (as constituted)
(Lt-Gen Alan Cunningham, after 26 November by Lt-Gen Neil Ritchie)

XXX Corps (Lt-Gen Willoughby Norrie)
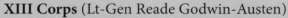
7th Armoured Division (Maj-Gen William Gott)
>Three armoured brigades (4th, 7th, 22nd)
>7th Support Group (artillery)
>Divisional troops
>>4th South African Armoured Car Regiment
>>King's Dragoon Guards
>>11th Hussars
>>1st LAA Regiment, RA

1st South African Division (Maj-Gen George Brink)
>Three infantry brigades (1st and 5th South African, 22nd Guards)

XIII Corps (Lt-Gen Reade Godwin-Austen)
2nd New Zealand Division (Maj-Gen Bernard Freyberg)
>Three infantry brigades (4th, 5th and 6th New Zealand)

4th Indian Infantry Division (Maj-Gen Frank Messervy)
>Three infantry brigades (5th, 7th and 11th Indian)
>Divisional troops
>>The Central India Horse (21st King George V's Own Horse) (recce)
>>Three field regiments, RA (1st, 25th and 31st)
>>1st Army Tank Brigade

Tobruk Fortress (Maj-Gen Ronald Scobie)
70th Infantry Division
>Three infantry brigades (14th, 16th and 23rd)
>Polish Independent Carpathian Rifle Brigade
>32nd Army Tank Brigade (Brig A.C. Willison)
>4th AA Brigade, RA (Brig John Muirhead)

Oasis Force (Brig Denys Reid)
>29th Indian Infantry Brigade
>6th South African Armoured Car Regiment

Army Reserve
2nd South African Division (Maj-Gen Isaac de Villiers)
>Three infantry brigades (3rd, 4th and 6th South African)

26 November thus cutting the Axis lines of communication. Rommel had attacked eastwards with Cairo in his sights – some of his advance troops actually crossed the border into Egypt in this 'Dash for the Wire' – but fuel and water were critically low and they were being harassed with increasing severity, so Rommel returned west and struck back hard soon forcing 70th Division back into Tobruk, though he still could not take the city.

The need to safeguard his remaining forces now prompted Rommel to withdraw to a defensive line at Gazala to the west of Tobruk, and following further skirmishes in western Cyrenaica during December, he withdrew again to El Agheila leaving Axis garrisons at Bardia and Halfaya, both of which surrendered soon after. Both sides had fought tenaciously but the Axis had suffered the more serious losses: 24,000 casualties, 32,000 prisoners, and nearly 400 tanks. The British had 18,000 casualties and lost nearly 300 tanks. Both sides now paused to resupply. British tank tactics needed rethinking in the face of such terrible losses. Although Tobruk had been relieved, the performance and price was considered too heavy and Auchinleck replaced Eighth Army commander Cunningham with Maj-Gen Neil Ritchie.

Above Left The Eighth Army shield – a yellow cross on a white background with black edging.

Below Afrika Korps palm and swastika crest, this on a PzKpfw IV.

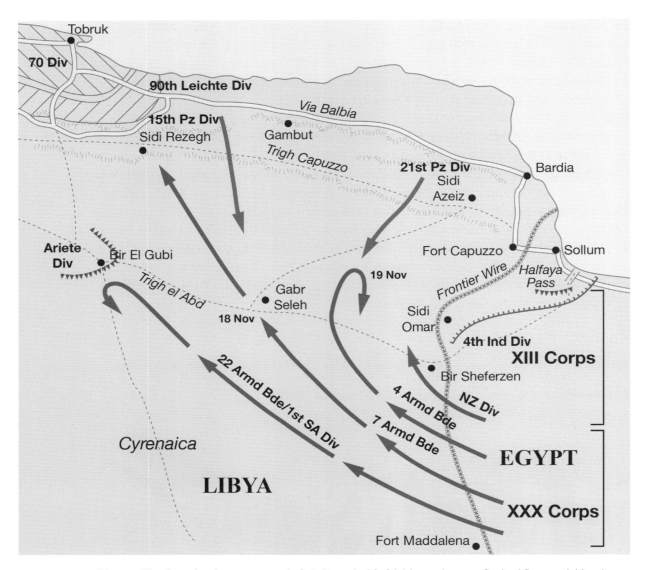

Above The British advance towards Sidi Rezegh, 18–21 November, outflanked Rommel. His slow reaction reflects the surprise attack, but he finally responded on 19 November and authorised a counterattack by 15th and 21st Panzer Divisions who clashed with 7th Armoured at Gabr Saleh.

Right A well-known feature of the area, the tomb of Sidi Rezegh still stands today in spite of the heavy fighting that swept around it. Both sides buried their dead nearby: this is a German cemetery. The Germans may account the battle a tactical victory but the toll on their armour by Eighth Army anti-tank gunners forced Rommel to retreat in the end.

GERMAN AND ITALIAN FORCES AT THE TIME OF 'CRUSADER'
Supreme Commander North Africa (General Ettore Bastico)

Italian XX Mobile Corps (Corpo d'Armata di Manovra)(Lt-Gen Gastone Gambara)
Corps troops
Three batteries of truck-mounted 102mm AA/AT guns
132nd Armoured Division Ariete (Gen Mario Balotta)
101st Motorised Division Trieste
Recce group (Raggruppamento Esplorante del Corpo d'Armata di Manovra)

Panzer Group Afrika (General der Panzertruppe Erwin Rommel)
Deutsches Afrika Korps (Generalleutnant Ludwig Crüwell)
15th Panzer Division (Generalmajor Walter Neumann-Silkow until
6 December (KIA), then Generalmajor Gustav von Vaerst)
21st Panzer Division (Generalmajor Johann von Ravenstein until
29 November (PoW), then Generalmajor Karl Böttcher)
Special Purpose Division Afrika (Renamed 90th Light Africa Division from
28 November 1941) (Generalmajor Max Sümmermann until
10 December (KIA), then Generalmajor Richard Veith)
55th Infantry Division Savona (General Fedele de Giorgis)

Italian XXI Corps (Lt-Gen Enea Navarini)
Corps troops
Various artillery
340th Frontier Guards Engineers Battalion
17th Infantry Division Pavia
25th Infantry Division Bologna
27th Infantry Division Brescia
102nd Motorised Division Trento

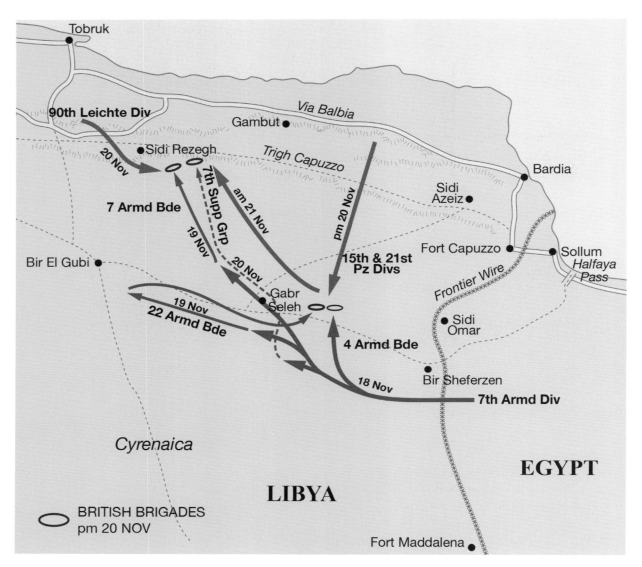

Map labels:
- Tobruk
- Via Balbia
- 90th Leichte Div
- Gambut
- Sidi Rezegh
- Trigh Capuzzo
- Bardia
- 20 Nov
- 7 Armd Bde
- 7th Supp Grp
- am 21 Nov
- Sidi Azeiz
- 19 Nov
- 20 Nov
- pm 20 Nov
- Fort Capuzzo
- Sollum
- Halfaya Pass
- Bir El Gubi
- 15th & 21st Pz Divs
- Gabr Seleh
- Frontier Wire
- 19 Nov
- 22 Armd Bde
- 4 Armd Bde
- Sidi Omar
- 18 Nov
- Bir Sheferzen
- 7th Armd Div
- Cyrenaica
- EGYPT
- LIBYA
- BRITISH BRIGADES pm 20 NOV
- Fort Maddalena

Above The battle of Sidi Rezegh, was intense and fought with great bravery on both sides. This map shows the position of the British brigades on the afternoon of 20 November, as Rommel counterattacked. The British lost 300 tanks, but the Germans were also hit hard and had fewer than 100 tanks left at the end of the engagement. An excellent example of the tenacious defence is the story of 3rd Field Regiment, the Transvaal Horse Artillery, who engaged elements of 15th and 21st Panzer Divisions over open sights on 23 November. The South African 5th Brigade suffered high losses – 224 killed, 379 wounded and 2,800 captured. The Germans lost 72 tanks.

Right Brig (later Maj-Gen) Jock Campbell (driving) won the VC at Sidi Rezegh. Tragically, in early 1942 after being promoted major-general and given command of British 7th Armoured Division, he was killed in a Jeep accident.

Above Left Rifleman John Beeley was in A Coy, 1st Bn, KRRC, one of two motor battalions in 7th Armoured's Support Group, when he won his VC. He is buried in Knightsbridge War Cemetery, Acroma, Libya. Today, his medal can be seen at the Royal Green Jackets Museum in Winchester.

Above Right Lt George Ward Gunn, VC, MC. Like Jock Campbell an Old Sedberghian, Gunn commanded A Troop of J Battery, RHA with four QF 2pdr anti-tank guns mounted on trucks. He won his VC posthumously, dying in the action which also saw his battery commander, Maj Bernard Pinney (son of Maj-Gen J. Pinney), recommended for the VC. Such was the valour showed by the men of J Battery that it was awarded the honorific 'Sidi Rezegh Battery' which it still sports.

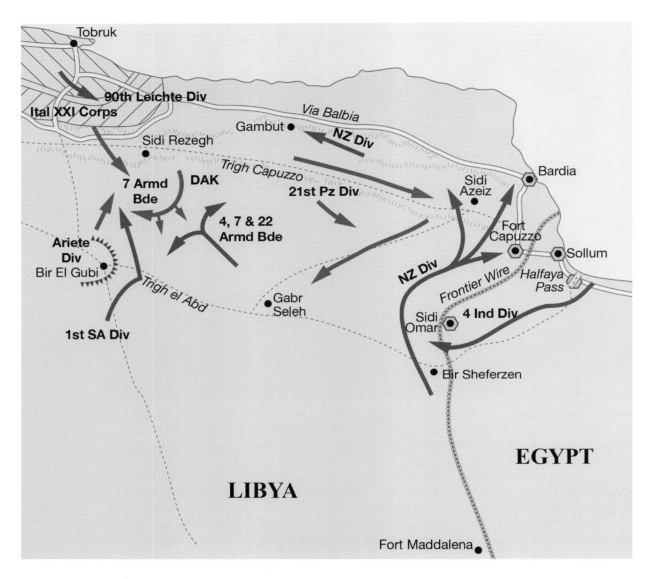

Above The Tobruk Garrison entered the battle on 22–23 November, trying to link up with the main attack. The Italian XX Mobile Corps, including the Ariete and Trieste divisions, were put under Rommel's command. 23 November 1941 was *Totensonntag* – Sunday of the Dead – and the Germans named the battle after it. The Germans inflicted heavy casualties on 7th Armoured Division which was forced to withdraw.

Right It may be posed but it shows well the arrangement of a 3in mortar pit – the crew was usually four: leader, gunner, loader and ammo bearer. Ammunition available was HE, smoke and illumination.

Above The difference in size between the Kübelwagen and SdKfz 7 is well illustrated here. The FP license plate of the Kübelwagen identifies that it is attached to the Feldpost and may be delivering letters. The Luftwaffe halftrack carries a gun crew and tows an 88mm Flak.

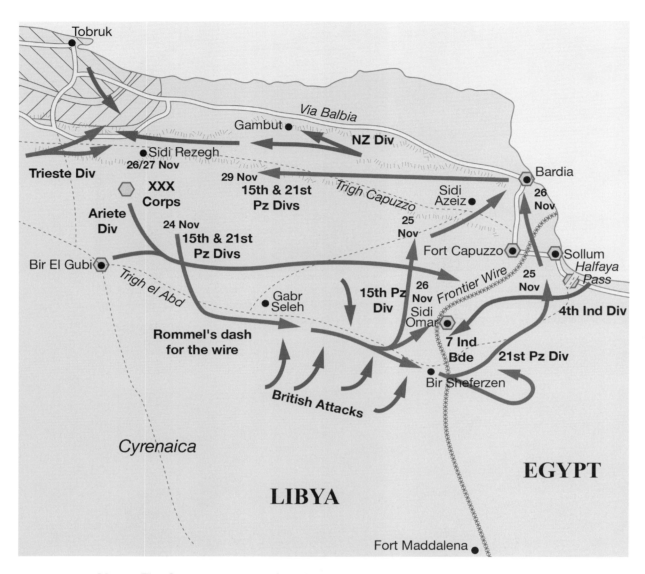

Tobruk

Via Balbia

Gambut

NZ Div

Sidi Rezegh
26/27 Nov

Trieste Div

Bardia
26
Nov

29 Nov
**15th & 21st
Pz Divs**

Trigh Capuzzo

Sidi
Azeiz

**XXX
Corps**

**Ariete
Div**

24 Nov
**15th & 21st
Pz Divs**

25
Nov

Fort Capuzzo

Sollum
Halfaya
Pass

Bir El Gubi

Trigh el Abd

Gabr
Seleh

**15th Pz
Div**

26
Nov

Sidi
Omar

Frontier Wire

25
Nov

4th Ind Div

**Rommel's dash
for the wire**

**7 Ind
Bde**

21st Pz Div

Bir Sheferzen

British Attacks

Cyrenaica

EGYPT

LIBYA

Fort Maddalena

Above The German attack east from 24 November – the 'Dash for the Wire' – failed and the Axis forces were forced to retreat, initially to deal with the break out from Tobruk, and were ultimately forced back to El Agheila. Casualty figures for the operation were high on both sides: British and Commonwealth losses amounted to 17,700; Axis forces to 24,500 – and even more after the frontier garrisons fell. Logistics issues were a significant factor in Rommel's defeat.

Opposite, Above A knocked out PzKpfw IV armed with a 75mm KwK 37 short-barrelled gun. The longer-gunned Ausf F2 didn't arrive in theatre until August 1942.

Right Another SdKfz 7/88mm combo. This gun has a number of kill rings on its barrel.

Medical supplies in the desert were as dependent on logistics as everything else. Ambulances were crucial to get casualties away from the battlefield – but the distances involved were long and only the seriously wounded were evacuated by air. The distance between a regimental aid post and casualty clearing station could be over a hundred miles and take two to three days for the wounded to reach. Further back would be medical centres. To carry the wounded the Austin K2/Y ambulance (**Opposite**), or 'Katy', was the mainstay of RAMC services – overall 13,000 were built. This one is crewed by medical orderlies from 7th Motorised Brigade.

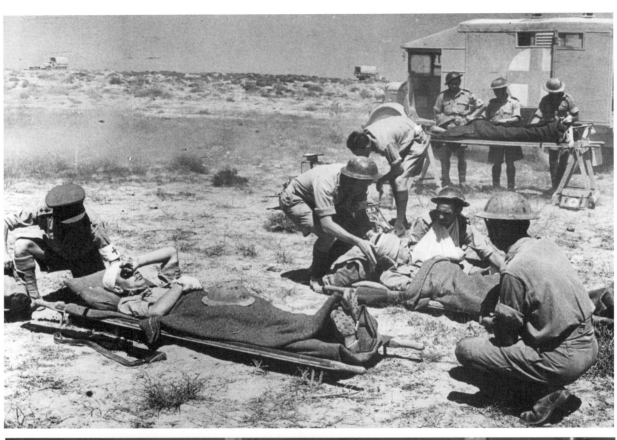

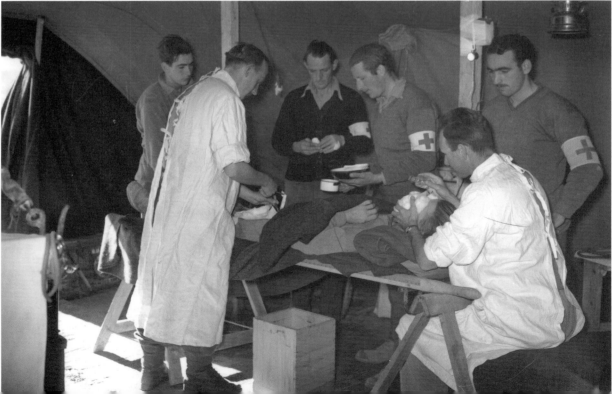

Left A 'Katy' waits to take the injured from a regimental aid post to a medical centre.

Below left Operating theatre in January 1941. One major medical development in the desert war was the use of penicillin in trials on wounded soldiers.

Right Most nurses in the desert were men although some women were involved at casualty clearing stations.

Below An MO in a Daimler Mk IB scout car gets directions from an Grant tank commander, 4th Armoured Brigade, 1943.

Top Rommel's drive to El Alamein was in two stages: first to Gazala (see maps on pages 98 and 100), and then after outflanking the British defensive line, east deep into Egypt.

Above Rommel used a Fiesler Fi156 Storch light aircraft from Kurierstaffel zbV Afrika to get around the battlefield.

Chapter Five

Rommel's Second Offensive

By January 1942 the Afrika Korps had been resupplied with another 55 tanks and Rommel counterattacked immediately. Once again the British were caught out by his speed and power, losing over a hundred tanks. He took Benghazi on 29 January and forced Eighth Army back to a defensive line at Gazala. More critical supplies then arrived in April giving him fresh impetus. The British, also resupplied, now had 900 tanks including 200 new American M3 mediums – Grants armed with a 75mm main gun – compared to 320 German tanks and 240 poor Italian ones.

On 26 May 1942 Rommel launched his new campaign with a feint – an assault, mostly by Italian infantry – on the central Gazalan fortifications. Meanwhile under the cover of darkness he moved the bulk of his armour (15th and 21st Panzers, 90th Light Division, and the Italian Ariete and Trieste Divisions) south of the British left flank to come up behind them for a dawn assault. Throughout the day a huge running battle ensued, with both sides taking heavy losses. It was the Germans' turn to feel impotent against armour, the Grants proving impossible to knock out except at close range. Renewing the attack the next day Rommel concentrated on encircling and destroying the British armour piecemeal, while repeated British counterattacks threatened to cut off and destroy his own forces.

Running low on fuel, Rommel then improvised a defensive position (the Cauldron) making use of British minefields to shield his western flank. On 30 May having refuelled he resumed the offensive, attacking westwards to link up with elements of Italian X Corps. On 10 June the hinge of the Allied defensive line (the Free French strongpoint at Bir Hakeim) fell and with his rear and the southern part the British line thus secured, Rommel shifted his attack north, relying once more on British minefields to protect his left flank. Sunday, 13 June, was a black day for the Eighth Army as the Germans – helped by their radio intelligence – broke down their defensive positions and threatened to cut off most of the army. There was no option but to begin a hasty retreat eastwards towards Egypt. The following day Axis forces reached the coast and trapped the remaining Allied troops at Gazala.

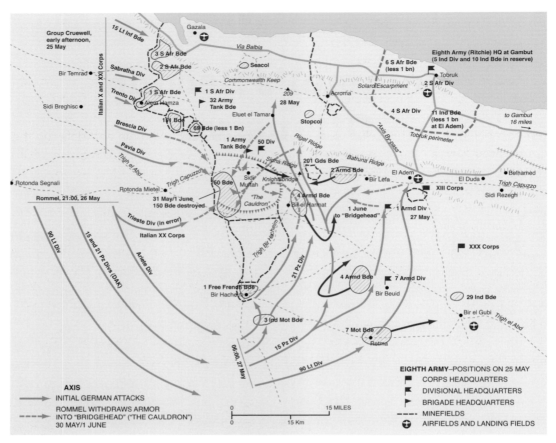

Group Cruewell, early afternoon, 25 May

Bir Temrad

Sidi Breghisc

Rotonda Segnali

Rommel, 21:00, 26 May

Italian X and XXI Corps

Sabratha Div
Trento Div
Brescia Div
Pavia Div

Trigh el Abd

90 Lt Div

15 and 21 Pz Divs (DAK)

Ariete Div

Italian XX Corps

Trieste Div (in error)

Trigh Capuzzo

Rotonda Mietel

15 Lt Inf Bde

3 S Afr Bde
2 S Afr Bde

Gazala

Via Balbia

Seacol

Commonwealth Keep

1 S Afr Bde
Alem Hamza

1 S Afr Div

209

1 S Afr Bde

32 Army Tank Bde

Eluet el Tamar

28 May

Stopcol

69 Bde (less 1 bn)

1 Bde

1 Army Tank Bde

50 Div

Sidra Ridge

Rigel Ridge

50 Bde

Sidi Muftah

Knightsbridge

"The Cauldron"

31 May/1 June 150 Bde destroyed

Bir el Harmat

Trigh Bir Hacheim

Trigh el Abd

06:00, 27 May

1 Free French Bde
Bir Hacheim

3 Ind Mot Bde

15 Pz Div

21 Pz Div

90 Lt Div

201 Gds Bde

Batruna Ridge

2 Armd Bde

Bir Lefa

4 Armd Bde

1 June to "Bridgehead"

4 Armd Bde

Bir Beuid

7 Mot Bde
Retma

Solaro Escarpment

Acroma

"Axis Bypass"

Tobruk perimeter

El Adem

El Duda

XIII Corps

1 Armd Div
27 May

7 Armd Div

XXX Corps

29 Ind Bde

Bir el Gubi

Trigh el Abd

Eighth Army (Ritchie) HQ at Gambut (5 Ind Div and 10 Ind Bde in reserve)

Tobruk

2 S Afr Div

6 S Afr Bde (less 1 bn)

4 S Afr Div

11 Ind Bde (less 1 bn at El Adem)

to Gambut 16 miles

Belhamed

Trigh Capuzzo

Sidi Rezegh

AXIS

→ INITIAL GERMAN ATTACKS

⇢ ROMMEL WITHDRAWS ARMOR INTO "BRIDGEHEAD" ("THE CAULDRON") 30 MAY/1 JUNE

0 ———— 15 MILES

0 ———— 15 Km

EIGHTH ARMY—POSITIONS ON 25 MAY

▪ CORPS HEADQUARTERS

▪ DIVISIONAL HEADQUARTERS

▸ BRIGADE HEADQUARTERS

--- MINEFIELDS

⊕ AIRFIELDS AND LANDING FIELDS

Taking advantage of the chaos and confusion Rommel now struck for Tobruk, assaulting on 20 June and succeeding by the next day. 32,000 defenders surrendered and huge quantities of valuable supplies fell into his hands. In acknowledgement, on 22 June Hitler promoted Rommel to Generalfeldmarschall. However, he would not countenance further resources being used in attempts to take Egypt and the Suez Canal.

On the British side, Auchinleck relieved Ritchie of command of Eighth Army and temporarily took over himself, preparing positions around El Alamein and delaying the Germans at Mersa Matruh on 28 June. Here, the 2nd New Zealand Division and 50th (Northumbrian) Infantry Division were almost trapped but managed to escape. Four divisions of X Corps were caught and ordered to break out, with the loss of 6,000 troops and 40 tanks. On 29 June the town fell and huge stockpiles of fuel and supplies along with hundreds of tanks and trucks were plundered.

Rommel pursued the Eighth Army to El Alamein, where the Quattara Depression creates a naturally defensive choke point that cannot be outflanked. He had only 100 tanks but hoped his momentum would win the day. Allied air superiority battered and contained 15th and 21st Panzers, while the 90th Light Division lost their way and were pinned down by artillery fire. After two days of no progress and with the Germans forces struggling to contain Auchinleck's counterattacks there was a pause in the fighting at the end of July as both sides rested and regrouped.

Left The battle of Gazala was Rommel's greatest triumph and Eighth Army's last major defeat in the desert war.

Below Left French light AA defences at Bir Hacheim – a 40mm Bofors gun.

Right The defence of Bir Hacheim – the key southern defensive box – was epic and saw the 1st Free French Brigade withstand 14 days of bombardment by Stukas and attacks by the German army. The defenders, under General Marie-Pierre Koenig, were eventually withdrawn under cover of night by 69 three-ton lorries and 33 ambulances manned by D Company, 2 Kings Royal Rifle Corps. Here Koenig is decorated by de Gaulle.

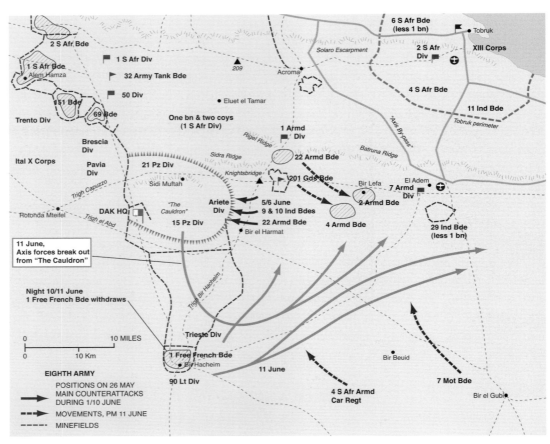

6 S Afr Bde
(less 1 bn)
● Tobruk
2 S Afr Bde
1 S Afr Bde
Alem Hamza
▲ 209
Acroma
2 S Afr Div
XIII Corps
● Eluet el Tamar
151 Bde
69 Bde
Trento Div
Brescia Div
Ital X Corps
Pavia Div
1 S Afr Div
32 Army Tank Bde
50 Div
One bn & two coys
(1 S Afr Div)
Solaro Escarpment
4 S Afr Bde
11 Ind Bde
Tobruk perimeter
21 Pz Div
Sidi Muftah ●
Knightsbridge
Rigel Ridge
1 Armd Div
Sidra Ridge
22 Armd Bde
201 Gds Bde
● Bir Lefa
Batruna Ridge
"Axis Bypass"
El Adem
7 Armd Div
Trigh Capuzzo
DAK HQ
"The Cauldron"
Ariete Div
5/6 June
9 & 10 Ind Bdes
22 Armd Bde
2 Armd Bde
4 Armd Bde
Rotonda Mteifel ●
Trigh el Abd
15 Pz Div
Bir el Harmat ●
29 Ind Bde
(less 1 bn)

11 June,
Axis forces break out
from "The Cauldron"

Trigh Bir Hacheim

Night 10/11 June
1 Free French Bde withdraws

Trieste Div

1 Free French Bde
● Bir Hacheim

90 Lt Div

11 June

● Bir Beuid

7 Mot Bde

4 S Afr Armd
Car Regt

● Bir el Gubi

0 — 10 MILES
0 — 10 Km

EIGHTH ARMY
POSITIONS ON 26 MAY
MAIN COUNTERATTACKS
DURING 1/10 JUNE
- - - ▶ MOVEMENTS, PM 11 JUNE
- - - - MINEFIELDS

Above Left Rommel's forces break out of the Cauldron and threaten to surround Eighth Army.

Left 21st Panzer Division PzKpfw III crew watch the German convoys move east.

Above While the battle of Gazala was a triumph for Rommel, the fighting certainly wasn't all one-sided. This Panzer crewman died alongside his PzKpfw III. The Germans and Italians had 400 tanks damaged or destroyed – less than half Eighth Army's losses.

Right German medical team in Tobruk.

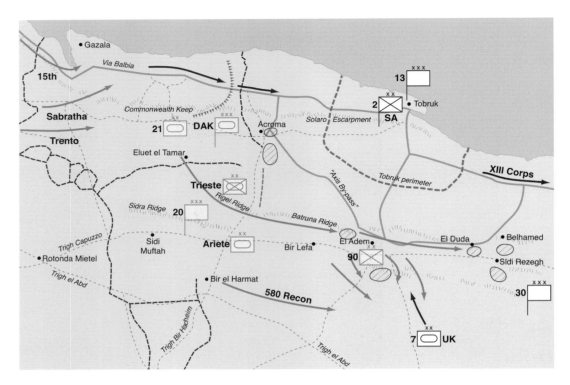

The following labels appear on the map:

- Gazala
- Via Balbia
- 15th
- 13 (XXX)
- Tobruk
- Commonwealth Keep
- 2 SA (XX)
- Sabratha
- 21 (XX)
- DAK (XXX)
- Acroma
- Solaro Escarpment
- Trento
- Eluet el Tamar
- "Axis By-pass"
- Tobruk perimeter
- XIII Corps
- Trieste (XX)
- Rigel Ridge
- Sidra Ridge
- 20 (XXX)
- Batruna Ridge
- Trigh Capuzzo
- Sidi Muftah
- Ariete (XX)
- Bir Lefa
- El Adem
- El Duda
- Belhamed
- Rotonda Mietel
- 90 (XX)
- Sidi Rezegh
- Trigh el Abd
- Bir el Harmat
- 580 Recon
- 30 (XXX)
- Trigh Bir Hacheim
- 7 (XX) UK
- Trigh el Abd

Above Tobruk fell on 20 June, a sickening blow for the British for whom it was a talisman after the last siege. As well as the supplies, the surrender of the 32,000-strong garrison and the boost to morale, the Germans gained a port that would significantly improve their supply lines – and Rommel was promoted Generalfeldmarscall by a grateful Führer.

Below Behind the Kübelwagen British and South African troops captured in Tobruk await transport to PoW camps.

British troops sift through the wreckage of a
German lorry hit during an air attack.

Above Eighth Army crest on the three-gallon fuel tank, this messenger sits on his BSA M20.

Below British AFVs used the No 19 wireless set from 1941 into the 1960s. They had three main components: an HF radio transmitter/receiver with a range of 50 miles; a VHF transmitter-receiver for short-range line-of-sight communications; and a separate unit provided crew communications.

As has already been discussed, British radio usage was intercepted by German surveillance and provided the Desert Fox with much information about troop movements. This was paricularly helpful during the battle of Gazala.

Right The No 11 set was used in British AFVs until replaced by the No 19 set.

Below The No 19 and 21 wireless sets were manufactured in Canada and the United States.

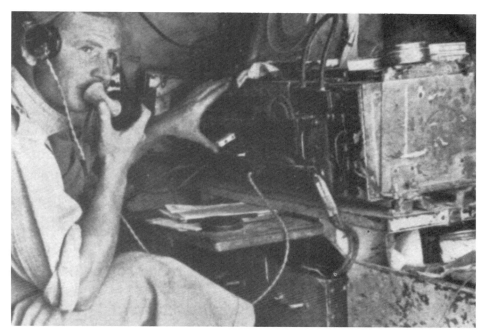

Left and Right While wireless technology improved greatly during the war, landlines were still vital. There was a signifigant landline between Alexandria and Mersah Matruh – the laying operations are shown here.

Below A portable telephone exchange based on a CMP Ford F60L.

Below Right Landlines were used by both sides. Here, Italian signalmen repair a break in the wire.

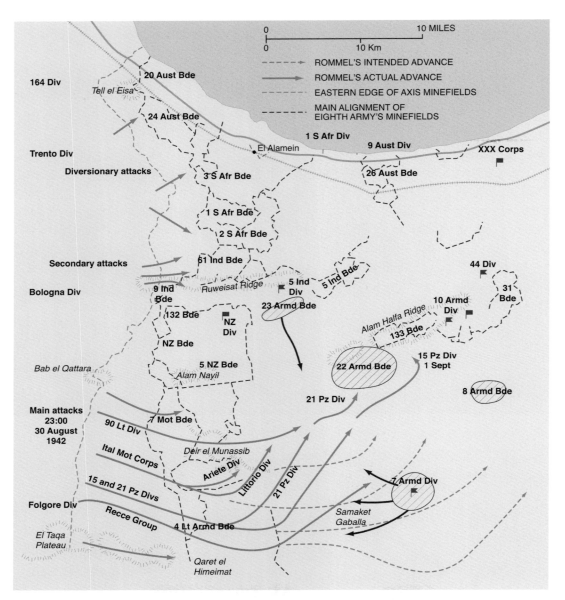

Above The battle of Alam Halfa was a major reverse for the Germans. The smashing success at Gazala, the arrival of new tanks and supplies – everything pointed to an opportunity to win the campaign in one last battle against the new, untried Eighth Army commander. What Rommel couldn't know is that for once the British knew what he intended rather than vice versa. Ultra intercepts allowed Montgomery to set a trap for the Axis forces and it was sprung at Alam Halfa Ridge.

Right Cometh the hour, cometh the man ... a classic portrait of Monty wearing his RTR beret in his command tank: a Grant named 'Monty'. He proved a capable and flexible commander, well liked by his men. In the background is his ADC, Captain John Posten, who commanded the tank.

Chapter Six

Monty Takes Command

On 8 August it was Auchinleck's turn to be replaced by General Harold Alexander (later Earl Alexander of Tunis and 17th governor general of Canada) as C-in-C Middle East. The Eighth Army had initially been assigned to General William 'Strafer' Gott but he died on 7 August when his aircraft was shot down and, after crash-landing, was strafed. In his stead General Bernard Montgomery was made the new commander. A cautious man, he succeeded in stalling for time from Churchill (who, as usual, was impatient for results) while he built up his forces and trained both fresh troops and also the old desert hands. There would be no more tank charges into the teeth of Rommel's 88s.

For his part, Rommel knew that with the hugely superior Allied supply chain, time was not on his side. Taking advantage of what supplies he had received in August – they had left him with 234 German and 281 Italian tanks – on 30 August he attacked. The German 15th and 21st Panzer and 90th Light Divisions and the Italian XX Motorised Corps assaulted the British southern flank – with the coast on one side and the desert on the other tactics were limited to such southern flanking manoeuvres. What Rommel didn't know was that the Allies' Ultra intercepts foretold his attack.

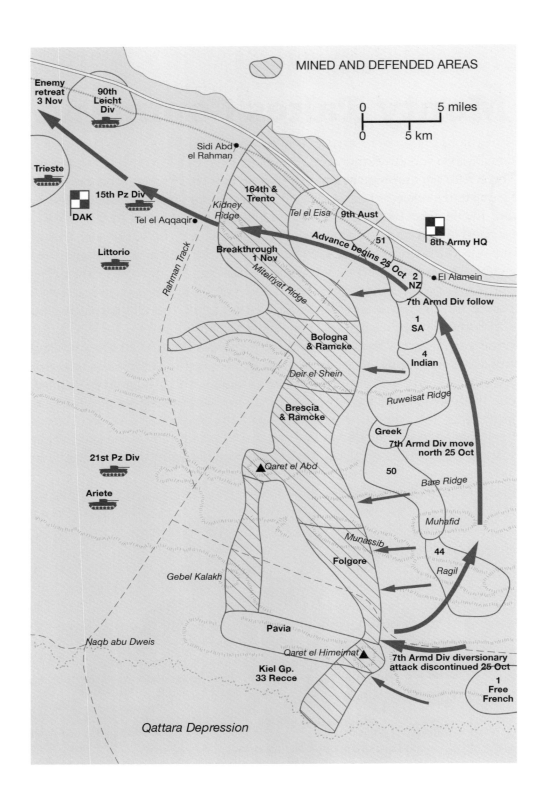

MINED AND DEFENDED AREAS

Enemy
retreat
3 Nov

90th
Leicht
Div

0   5 miles

0   5 km

Trieste

Sidi Abd
el Rahman

164th &
Trento

15th Pz Div

DAK

Kidney
Ridge

Tel el Eisa

9th Aust

8th Army HQ

Tel el Aqqaqir

51

Advance begins 25 Oct

Littorio

Rahman Track

Breakthrough
1 Nov

Miteiriyat Ridge

2
NZ

El Alamein

7th Armd Div follow

1
SA

Bologna
& Ramcke

4
Indian

Deir el Shein

Ruweisat Ridge

Brescia
& Ramcke

Greek

7th Armd Div move
north 25 Oct

21st Pz Div

50

Bare Ridge

Qaret el Abd

Muhafid

Ariete

Munassib

44

Folgore

Ragil

Gebel Kalakh

Pavia

Naqb abu Dweis

Qaret el Himeimat

7th Armd Div diversionary
attack discontinued 25 Oct

Kiel Gp.
33 Recce

1
Free
French

Qattara Depression

110

Montgomery set a trap for the Desert Fox, fortifying the Alam Halfa ridge with the 44th Division and positioning the 7th Armoured Division close by to the south. Rommel's forces soon got bogged down in the extensive minefields and unstable desert, whilst being attacked by aircraft and artillery. Increasing Allied air superiority and German lack of fuel were critical factors and when the attack stalled having suffered 3,000 casualties and lost 50 tanks, Rommel withdrew. On 3 September, 2nd New Zealand Division and 7th Armoured Division attacked to the north but were repulsed by a fierce 90th Light Division rearguard. An ill Rommel, worn out by the long campaign and fearing that it could not be won with the meagre resources he had left, flew home to Germany to recuperate. Eighth Army had won a significant victory.

Monty remained cautious and took his time to prime his hugely superior forces. Finally, on 23 October 1942 he began his offensive with a massive 1,000-gun artillery barrage followed by an infantry assault across a narrow stretch of the German minefields. This turned into a bitter hand-to-hand infantry battle, and when his replacement as commander of Panzerarmee Afrika, Gen Georg Stumme died while reviewing the front, Rommel rushed back to Africa. He arrived with the German forces in a parlous state, made worse as tanker after tanker of precious fuel was destroyed by RAF action. Realising that if he did nothing, his army would be constricted, Rommel immediately counterattacked and tried to take the initiative. In spite of his best efforts, Eighth Army's defence held him off and four days of brutal attritional fighting left Rommel on the verge of defeat.

Montgomery launched Operation 'Supercharge' on 2 November using two armoured and two infantry divisions preceded by another artillery barrage. Rommel counterattacked again, but in the end the numbers told and with only some 35 tanks remaining, he ordered his forces to withdraw. He was stunned when the Führer commanded him not to retreat and, though he briefly complied, he soon ignored the order as Montgomery burst through his defences threatening to surround him so that he even had to abandon unmotorised troops.

Finally on 4 November Hitler relented but the retreat of the Afrika Korps was already underway. Aided by bad weather grounding Allied aircraft, they continued to retreat west fighting a series of delaying actions at Halfaya Pass, Sollum, Mersa Brega and El Agheila, heading for Gabes gap in Tunisia. Tobruk was recaptured on 13 November. By now the Germans fought in small combat groups outnumbered by massively superior British and Commonwealth forces who had complete air supremacy. Sirte fell, then Tripoli. Finally in March 1943 the Axis troops withdrew to the heavily defended Mareth Line, to await the inevitable British attack.

Left El Alamein, the turning point of the desert war if not the war itself. After so many defeats, Eighth Army finally saved Alexandria – only 66 miles distant – and the Suez Canal.

EIGHTH ARMY AT EL ALAMEIN (Lt-Gen Bernard Montgomery)

Under direct Army Command
1st Army Tank Brigade (minesweeping Matildas, to XXX Corps)
1st Armoured Brigade
2nd and 12th Anti-Aircraft Brigades
21st Indian Infantry Brigade (HQ protection, camouflage and guard duties)
Varous Army Troops inc 8th Army Signals, RSigs

British X Corps (Lt-Gen Herbert Lumsden)
Varous Corps Troops inc RSigs

1st Armoured Division (Maj-Gen Raymond Briggs)
2nd Armoured Brigade
7th Motor Brigade
Hammerforce (attached from 8th Armoured Division)
Minefield Task Force attached to Hammerforce for mine clearance

British 10th Armoured Division (Maj-Gen Alexander Gatehouse)
Two armoured brigades (8th and 24th, latter attached from 8th Armoured Division)
133rd Infantry Brigade (attached from 44th Infantry Division)
Minefield Task Force (Attached to 133 Bde for mine clearance)

British 8th Armoured Division (Maj-Gen Charles Gairdner)

XIII Corps (Lt-Gen Brian Horrocks)
Varous Corps Troops inc RSigs

7th Armoured Division (Maj-Gen A.F. Harding)
4th Light Armoured Brigade
24th Armoured Brigade
1st Free French Brigade Group

44th (Home Counties) Division (Maj-Gen Ivor Hughes)
Two infantry brigades (131st and 132nd)

50th (Northumbrian) Division (Maj-Gen John S. Nichols)
Two infantry brigades (69th and 151st)
1st Greek Brigade
2nd Free French Brigade Group

British XXX Corps (**Lt-Gen** Oliver Leese)
Varous Corps Troops inc RSigs and 23rd Armoured Brigade (Brig George W. Richards) in reserve

1st South African Division (Maj-Gen Dan Pienaar)
Three infantry brigades (South African 1st, 2nd and 3rd)

2nd New Zealand Division (Lt-Gen Bernard Freyberg)
Two infantry brigades (New Zealand 5th and 6th)
9th Armoured Brigade

4th Indian Infantry Division (Maj-Gen Francis Tuker)
Three infantry brigades (Indian 5th, 7th and 161st)

9th Australian Division (Maj-Gen Leslie Morshead)
Three infantry brigades (Australian 20th, 24th and 26th)

British 51st (Highland) Infantry Division (Maj-Gen Douglas Wimberley)
Three infantry brigades (152nd, 153rd and 154th)

PANZER ARMY AFRIKA AT EL ALAMEIN (GFM Erwin Rommel)

Army troops

German 90th Light Afrika Division Generalmajor Ernst Strecker)

German 164th Light Afrika Division (Generalleutnant-Carl-Hans Lungershausen)

Ramcke Parachute Brigade (Generalmajor Hermann-Bernhard Ramcke)

Deutsches Afrika Korps (Generalleutnant Wilhelm Ritter von Thoma)
German 15th Panzer Division (Generalmajor Gustav von Vaerst)

German 21st Panzer Division (Generalmajor Heinz von Randow)

Italian Army Africa (Marshal Ettore Bastico)
16th Motorised Division Pistoia (Maj-Gen Giuseppe Falugi)

136th Infantry Division Giovani Fascisti

Italian X Corps (Lt-Gen Edoardo Nebba; Maj-Gen Enrico Frattini in temporary command to October 26)
9th Bersaglieri Regiment

Italian 27th Infantry Division Brescia (Maj-Gen Brunetto Brunetti)

Italian 17th Infantry Division Pavia (Brig Nazzareno Scattaglia)

Italian 185th Parachute Division Folgore (Maj-Gen Enrico Frattini)

Italian XX Motorized Corps (Lt-Gen Giuseppe de Stephanis)

Italian 132nd Armoured Division Ariete (Maj-Gen Francesco Arena)

Italian 133rd Armoured Division Littorio (Maj-Gen Gervasio Bitossi)

Italian 101st Motorised Division Trieste (Brig Francisco La Ferla)

Italian XXI Corps (Lt-Gen Enea Navarini; Maj-Gen Alessandro Gloria in temporary command to October 26)
7th Bersaglieri Regiment

Italian 102nd Motorised Division Trento (Brig Giorgio Masina)

Italian 25th Infantry Division Bologna (Maj-Gen Alessandro Gloria)

Italian troops head towards Alam Halfa.

Above Rommel had 'Max' and 'Moritz', the Mammuts (Mammoths), AEC Dorchester 4x4 armoured command vehicles captured from the British; Monty also had a similar model.

Opposite, Above and Below Monty put himself about, making himself visible to his men. He wrote later 'I soon learned that the arrival of the double-badged beret on the battlefield was a help – they knew that I was about, that I was taking an intense and personal interest in their doings, and that I was not just sitting about somewhere safe in the rear issuing orders.'

Above Digging in the desert wasn't a question of shifting sand. So much of the desert is stony that often only sangars were practical.

Below Long-barrelled 75mm PzKpfw IVs proved hugely effective in the desert, but the Germans had too few of them. During the attritional stage of the battle of El Alamein, by 27 October the German Panzers had been reduced to 114 runners and the Italians to 206; the British had lost 215.

Italian infantry with an 47/32 M35 anti-tank gun.

Above and Left The preliminary artillery barrage at the start of Operation 'Lightfoot' involved around a thousand guns firing from 21:40 to 22:00.

Below To clear the way the operation started with sappers using mine detectors or flail tanks (see next page).

Above A British Crusader passes a brewed-up PzKpfw IV at the end of the battle.

Opposite, Above In 1941 South African Maj A. S. J. du Toit, devised a mine-clearing device although the Matilda Scorpion – as seen here – was the work of Capt Norman Berry, RAOC. 32 Scorpions of 42nd and 44th RTR were involved in the battle of El Alamein.

Opposite, Below A Marmon Herrington Mk III, a South African-manufactured armoured car, advances under fire.

Right Generalmajor Georg von Bismarck, commander of 21st Panzer Division, died on 31 August 1942 during the battle of Alam Halfa – one of the problems for thrusting generals in the desert war. Georg Stumme, then commanding the Axis forces, died of a heart attack when under fire on 24 October at the start of the battle of El Alamein.

Below Equality! M4A1 and a few M4A2 Shermans arrived in the desert in time for El Alamein and gave the Eighth Army a tank that could match anything the Germans had, until the Tiger arrived.

Top The name of this small, dusty station resounds through the history of World War II: El Alamein.

Above At Alamein Eighth Army had around 195,000 men ranged against around 110,000 Axis troops.

Above Probably posed and often captioned as a mine explosion, the Eighth Army lorried infantry were shelled as they made their way through the belt of minefields during the breakout.

Below The Germans were always good at reusing captured material. This is a Soviet 75mm gun used in an anti-tank role.

The Axis lost a lot of valuable equipment as it retreated back towards Mareth, including over 450 tanks, either knocked out or abandoned, and over a thousand guns. Here a PzKpfw III (**Above**) and one of the valuable 88mm twin Flak and anti-tank guns (**Below**) which had caused havoc to both British and, after their arrival in theatre, US tankers. Because they were retreating the Germans weren't able to reclaim the vehicles from the battlefield, something they usually did well; the British, however, recovered many of their losses.

The Axis army began to disintegrate after a week of heavy fighting and the prisoners and wounded made their way back to Eighth Army's rear. The joy after victory was unconfined, and church bells rang in Britain for the first time since Dunkrk.

Above Note the wounded prisoner on the Universal carrier.

Below and Opposite, Below Who said it was hot in the desert? Note all the overcoats.

Opposite, Above Jean Pallud identifies these German troops as men of Panzergrenadier-Regiment 382 who lost 'nearly all of two battalions' in the opening attack. They are passing an abandoned German 50mm anti-tank gun.

Left On 23 January 1943 Eighth Army took Tripoli (a surrender ceremony took place at Porta Benito). On the 26th there was a victory parade with the band of the 51st Highland Division providing the music (**Above left** Monty inspecting men of the division). The 51st had led the way at El Agheila and Buerat. Monty rode in a Humber Super Snipe. The Axis delaying actions (**Below**) meant that Eighth Army were running short of supplies that the capture of Tripoli alleviated as — while the port was destroyed by the departing Germans — lighters were still able to land.

Above Long lines of German prisoners.

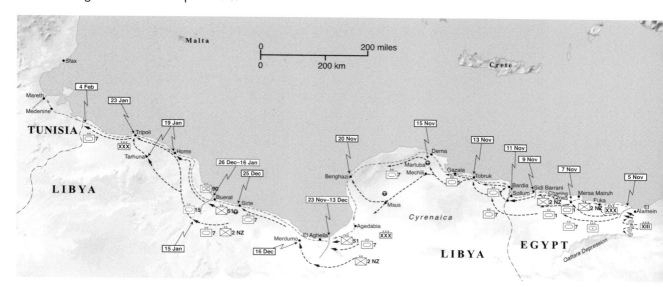

The Desert Air Force (commanded by AVM Sir Arthur Coningham) outperformed its German equivalent. One of the main reasons for this was the way that air-ground cooperation was perfected – a skill that the RAF would pass on to the USAAF and would be shown to great effect in Normandy. AM Sir Arthur Tedder was fundamental in this, serving first as deputy and then as Commander of British Air Forces in the Middle East. His reorganisations created a tactical air force in the western desert; a separate command to provide maintenance; division of ground and air elements of each squadron so that maintenance support could leapfrog ahead of their aircraft; and finally the coordination of fighters and army AA guns.

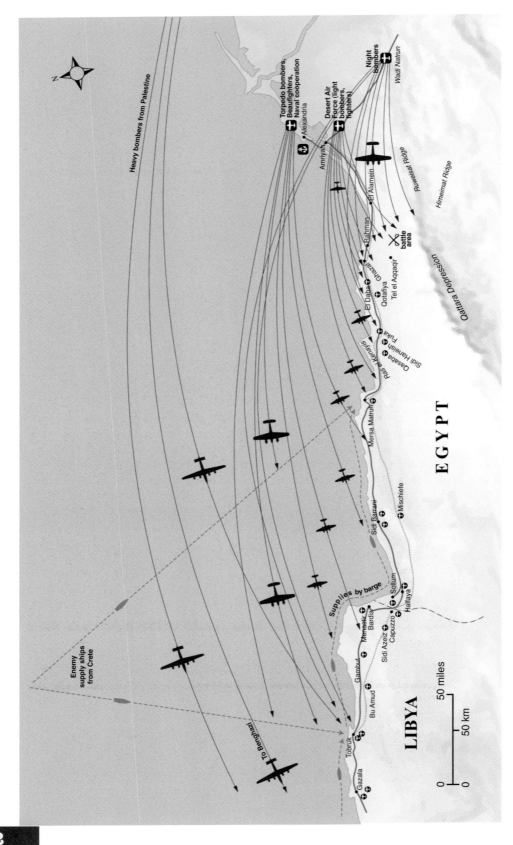

The Germans' logistics were a nightmare. Even when sufficient materiel reached Tripoli (their major port) it needed to be moved to the front by truck. El Alamein is 1,200 miles from Tripoli so it is not surprising to hear that estimates put truck fuel consumption accounted for up to half of the fuel supply. And the closer the trucks got to the front, the closer they got to the RAF as this diagram shows. The British were better at this, partly because they had built railways and pipelines and had better naval assets.

Right Operations in North Africa by Allied air forces. A light bomber of the South African air force comes in to bomb a large enemy barracks in Mareth village. Low clouds are above the target area. In the right foreground, bombs dropped by the previous aircraft can be seen exploding on the target. The aircraft is a Douglas A-20 – named the Boston III in Commonwealth service. They arrived in theatre and saw action from February 1942. By the time of El Alamein the Desert Air Force had 29 squadrons (nine of which were South African) flying over 1,500 aircraft.

Above Linkup! British and American troops meet on the Gafsa–Gabès road on 7 April 1943. Axis surrender in North Africa was only a month away. They may not have realised it, but the arrival of the US Army signalled the death knell of the Third Reich. Over the next year, as first Sicily and then southern Italy fell to the Allies, the preparations for an invasion of France were made. The Germans may have won tactical victories over the Allies after this, but they didn't make any impression on the grand strategy. The war may not have been won in Africa, but after their success they knew that they could win.

Below White Beach, Bou Zedjar, Algeria. Operation 'Torch' took place with minimal resistance, although the Germans rushed reinforcements to North Africa.

Chapter Seven

First Victory

On 8 October 1942 the Allied landings in northwest Africa – Operation 'Torch' – surprised the Germans, who were now trapped in Tunisia between two armies. After having been denied suitable troop levels for so long, Hitler rushed in reinforcements but they were too few and too late. On 19–25 February, Rommel turned briefly to maul the inexperienced American forces at the Kasserine Pass in what would turn out to be his last successful battle. He then turned back to face the Eighth Army on the Mareth Line. His final offensive on 6 March was at Medenine using 10th, 15th and 21st Panzer Divisions. Forewarned by Ultra intercepts, Eighth Army had prepared a killing zone bristling with anti-tank guns – much as the Afrika Korps had done so many times to the British earlier in the campaign – and after losing many tanks and men Rommel called off the assault. On 9 March he was ordered back to Germany and never returned. Overall command of the Axis forces passed to the Italian General Messe as most of the remaining units were Italian.

Taking advantage of his overwhelming air superiority, on 19 March Montgomery opened Operation 'Pugilist' with bombers and a barrage before attacking the central part of Mareth Line defences. 50th (Northumbrian) Division penetrated the Italian line near Zarat, but the 15th Panzer Division counterattacked and recaptured lost ground. However, a British LRDG unit under Capt N.P. Wilder had found an alternative route and on 21 March, 2nd New Zealand Division – beefed up to corps status – bypassed completely the Mareth Line by hooking round it through Wilder's Gap to the west and assaulted the surprised German defences at the Tebaga Gap. On 23 March Montgomery committed his reserve – 1st Armoured Division – to reinforce the New Zealand troops, while Indian 4th Division attacked simultaneously from the western end of the Mareth Line.

By the 25th they had successfully overrun it and the following day saw the launch of Operation 'Supercharge II' to exploit this penetration. British tanks pushed through the Tebaga Gap and approached El Hamma to the north. 15th Panzer Division began to counter this offensive while Axis troops started retreating from the Mareth Line towards Wadi Akarit (the original line favoured by Rommel who had viewed the Mareth as vulnerable). Although they stopped the British briefly at El Hamma they could not contain the New Zealand Division from breaking through. By 28 March most Axis

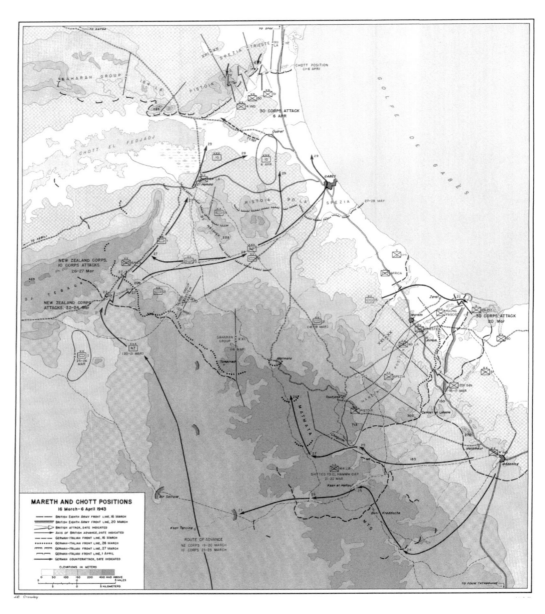

MARETH AND CHOTT POSITIONS
16 March–6 April 1943

Rommel was unable to hold the Eighth Army at the Mareth Line, Operation 'Supercharge II' outflanking the defensive positions and the heavy fighting that ensued saw 4,000 Eighth Army casualties but much higher losses on the Axis side. Over 7,500 entered captivity of which 2,500 were Germans. North of Wadi Akarit, Patton's II Corps had held an attack at El Guettar by 10th Panzer Division but had been unable to follow-up. The battle at Wadi Akarit on 6/7 April, however, saw Eighth Army break through. First DAF bombers pounded the defenses, then the position was taken and, finally, German counterattacks were beaten off. The Axis retreat looked more like a rout.

troops had been evacuated and the New Zealanders went on to take Gabès the next day. By 31 March British troops occupied Cap Serrat and Operation 'Supercharge II' was successfully concluded. After stubborn resistance, on 6–7 April at Wadi Akarit, the Axis forces fell back to their final defensive positions at Enfidaville. With complete naval and air supremacy, plus the Ultra intercepts, the Allies dominated the Mediterranean and isolated the remaining Axis Forces in Africa from all hope of resupply or escape.

With almost no ammunition, fuel or food the entire Axis force of 248,000 men, including the recently arrived reinforcements, surrendered on 13 May 1943. A vital first victory had been achieved against the Axis powers and Churchill's famous phrase caught the moment: 'the end of the beginning.' Rommel was devastated to lose his beloved Afrika Korps but only to his command staff did the Führer acknowledge the setback. His attention was firmly fixed on his prime objective: victory against Soviet Russia. For the Eighth Army, having fought so long and hard, it was a vindication of their tenacity and their freshly promoted and decorated commander's determination; but the show was by no means over. Less than two months later in July 1943 they would be fighting in another brutal new campaign.

Most assessments of Eighth Army and its adversaries concentrate on the deficiencies of British armour and anti-tank capabilities, the poor tactics that were employed, and the superiority of the *German* troops, equipment and – above all – commander. The Desert Fox may have been an excellent tactician and a dashing commander, but he was also prone to blame his Italian allies for defeats, sacrifice their men to protect his own, over-extend his supply lines and hope that momentum and his excellent armoured units could 'bounce' the Eighth Army by sheer momentum alone. Had he waited for Malta to be overwhelmed – as Kesselring proposed – the battles in autumn 1942 might have been less one-sided.

On the other side, the position of British forces in North Africa was often worsened by external events: Churchill removing forces for use in Greece or Crete; a revolt in Iraq and the Vichy French in Syria that led to the formation of Ninth Army in Palestine and Tenth in Iraq. But as soon as the British won the intelligence war, made better use of their aerial assets and concentrated their superiority in numbers under a charismatic and talented general and gave him sufficient time to do his job, the German African sideshow was over.

Eighth Army's success, however, was not just down to numbers: the bravery shown throughout the campaign – particularly by its powerful contingents from Australia, India, South Africa and New Zealand or as shown by the Free French at Bir Hakeim – often held off the enemy when it seemed that they would roll into Cairo and Alexandria. They stuck to their job, often poorly armed, sometimes poorly led, against a tough opponent and came out on top.

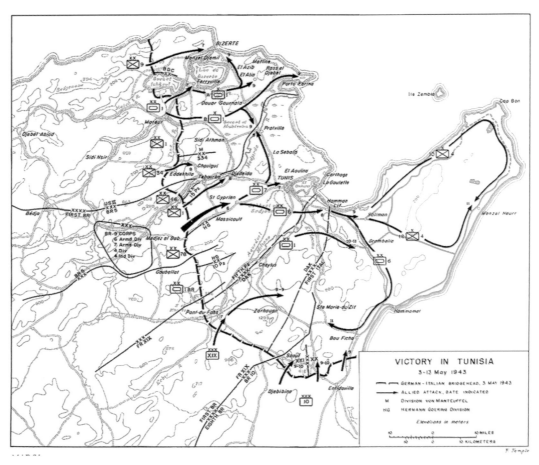

VICTORY IN TUNISIA
3–13 May 1943

GERMAN - ITALIAN BRIDGEHEAD, 3 MAY 1943
ALLIED ATTACK, DATE INDICATED
M   DIVISION VON MANTEUFFEL
HG HERMANN GOERING DIVISION
Elevations in meters

10   0   10 MILES
10   0   10 KILOMETERS

Left Victory in Tunisia was speeded up by the arrival of more British – in the form of First Army – and American troops.

Below left Italian troops guarded by their American captors pass a German 75mm gun.

Above and Below Tigers in Africa: these (**Above**) were knocked out by an air strike. This one (**Below**), being inspected by HM King George VI, was captured by First Army.

Not only taken prisoner but subjected to bagpipes as well. One of the lesser war crimes documented in the war!

Faces of victory: a gunner holds a 25-pounder projectile (**Above**) and V for Victory signs in Tunis while making use of a German Zundapp KS750 motorcycle and sidecar liberated from the the Afrika Korps.

Further Reading

Bender, Roger James, and Law, Richard D.: *Uniforms, Organization and History of the Afrikakorps*; R. James Bender Publishing, 1973.

Chamberlain, Peter, and Doyle, Hilary L.: *Encyclopedia of German Tanks of World War II*; Arms and Armour Press, 1978.

Ford, Ken: *Campaign 158 El Alamein 1942*; Osprey, 2005.

Ford, Ken: *Campaign 220 Operation Crusader 1941*; Osprey, 2010.

Forty, George: *Afrika Korps at War I and II*; Ian Allan Ltd, 1977, 1978.

Forty, George: *Desert Rats at War*; Air Sea Media, 2014.

Forty, George: *The Armies of Rommel*; Arms and Armour Press, 1997.

Forty, George: *The Desert War*; Alan Sutton, 2002.

Hogg, Ian V.: *German Artillery of World War Two*; Greenhill Books, 1997.

Lannoy, François de: *Afrikakorps The Libya-Egypt Campaign*; Heimdal, 2002.

Lucas, James: *Panzer Army Afrika*; Macdonald & Janes, 1977.

Milsom, John, and Chamberlain, Peter: *German Armoured Cars of World War Two*; Arms and Armour Press, 1974.

Pallud, Jean Paul: *The Desert War Then and Now*; After the Battle, 2012.

Perrett, Bryan: *Armour in Action 2 The Matilda*; Ian Allan Ltd, 1973.

Scipion, Jacques, and Bastien, Yves: *Afrikakorps Tropical Uniforms of the German Army 1940–1945*; Histoire & Collections, 1996.

Spaulding, Lt-Col David E.: *Early North African Campaigns 1940–1942*; US Army War College, 1992.

Verney, General G.L.: *The Desert Rats*; Hutchinson, 1954.

Wilkinson-Latham, John: *Men at Arms Montgomery's Desert Army*; Osprey, 1977.

Windrow, Martin: *Men at Arms Rommel's Desert Army*; Osprey, 1977.